Other books by Rev. Donald H. Hilton:

Boy into Man
Girl into Woman

Published by Denholm House Press

WORDS TO SHARE

An anthology of poetry and prose for use in Christian education and worship

DONALD H. HILTON

DENHOLM HOUSE PRESS

Robert Denholm House,
Nutfield, Redhill, Surrey, RH1 4HW

First published in 1974

ISBN 0 85213 128 3

Printed in Great Britain by
Ebenezer Baylis & Son Limited
The Trinity Press, Worcester, and London

CONTENTS

INTRODUCTION

This anthology of poetry and prose is offered as resource material for Christian education and worship. The compiler has chiefly had in mind Junior departments in churches and Middle Schools but also the wider needs of family worship in church.

The themes under which the material is collected begin with experiences which are immediate to the children and move out in widening circles to the family, the cycle of the year and the created world. It is hoped that this pattern will make the anthology sufficiently interesting for children to use the book for personal reading also.

Many of the quotations offer an overtly Christian interpretation of human experience; many of them are neither specifically Christian nor religious. However, the selection has been restricted to items which, whether expressed in formal religious language or not, interlock with religious experience and illuminate daily life.

Each of the six main sections is preceded by a comment which seeks to set the quotations in the context of our theological and educational task.

Two indexes are given at the back of the book. One is an index of first lines and the other shows material suitable for prayers. Each of the thirty-six sub-sections offers Bible references appropriate to the theme, and a cross-reference to items which, though placed under one theme, are relevant to another.

DONALD H. HILTON

Norwich
1974

THIS IS MY LIFE

THEME COMMENT

From the confused impressions of very early childhood a baby gradually learns the geography of his own body and surroundings. From a mass of blurred images, recognisable features emerge which he will later be able to identify as 'cot', 'Mum', 'fingers' etc. There is a progression from unrelated experiences, through recognisable experiences and the ability both to anticipate and reflect on them, to an awareness of experiences so persistent that they can be named. Discovery and learning has begun.

'Self' becomes distinct from other animate and inanimate objects. The young child is egocentric not out of wicked selfishness but because he must begin from his immediate experience in his exploration of the world. We must distinguish between selfishness and self-awareness.

From involvement with other people comes the gradual awareness that there is a 'self' in others which not only deserves respect but can meet the self in us. In the age-group for which this anthology is prepared the early promptings of this response are made, providing the challenge out of which can emerge a lively interest in the 'other' we call God.

Curiosity is a major asset of childhood and is a formative influence for the whole of life. The child's fields of exploration are his own life, other people, the world around and God Himself.

Me

SEE ALSO:
20,29a,31b,39b,
44b,61b,63a,71c,
156b,157b,160

(*a*) Holy God, who madest me
And all things else to worship Thee;
Keep me fit in mind and heart,
Body and soul to take my part.
Fit to stand, fit to run,
Fit for sorrow, fit for fun,
Fit to work and fit to play,
Fit to face life day by day:
Holy God, who madest me,
Make me fit to worship Thee.

ANON

(*b*) Lord, I love to stamp and shout
Testing lungs and muscles out;
Other times I curl up still
Dreaming till I've had my fill:
Still as mouse, or ranting free –
What is it that makes me me?

Lord, I love to watch things fly
Whizzing, zooming, flashing by;
Engines, aircraft, speedboats, cars,
Spacecraft shooting to the stars:
As I learn, and think and grow
Let my life say, "Go, man, go!"

Lord, I love to probe and pry,
Seeking out the reason why;
Looking inside things and out
Finding what they're all about;
Make me curious to find
What will bless, not hurt, mankind.

Lord, I'm many things and one
Though my life's not long begun;
You alone my secret see
What I am cut out to be:
Take this life – it's almost new –
Make your dream for it come true.

IAN M. FRASER

(*a*) I can climb the highest mountain,
Sail across the widest sea,
Now that I've discovered
That I'm happy to be me.

I can study mathematics,
Be a man of high degree,
Now I've solved the puzzle
That I'm happy to be me.

I can make the finest music,
Write a book of poetry,
Now I've learned the lesson
That I'm happy to be me.

I can do the things I dreamed of,
Live a life that's grand and free,
Now I've found the secret
That I'm happy to be me.

JOHN EDWARDS

(*b*) I am trying to recall, as I write this, what I meant in my young boyhood by praying. I think I meant a process in which getting outside oneself, getting inside oneself, communing with God (very vaguely felt as something all pervading and good), communing with the leaves and the sky and London and the dahlias in the market gardens, flinging up one's arms and expressing gratitude for the joy of living as one sniffed the air, and making up one's mind to be a better boy so that one shouldn't feel shut out from all these cleannesses and beauties – I think I meant a process in which things of this kind and others like them were somehow all mixed up.

VICTOR GOLLANCZ

(*a*) Lord of the loving heart,
May mine be loving too.
Lord of the gentle hands,
May mine be gentle too.
Lord of the willing feet,
May mine be willing too.
So may I grow more like to thee
In all I say and do.

From *Time and Again* prayers

(*b*) Grant us that we may never
forget, O Lord, that every man
is the son of a King.

AN OLD JEWISH PRAYER

(*c*) You have searched the depth of my being, O GOD,
you know all about me –
when I'm resting,
when I'm working.
You have probed my deepest intentions,
tracking out the road I take
and my camping grounds.
You know me through and through,
understanding better than I what I'm trying to say.

You have laid siege to me
behind me and before me;
you have put your hand on my shoulder –
I don't know why.
All this is beyond me,
out of my reach
I can't grasp it.

from Psalm 139.1–6 (*Winding Quest*, ALAN T. DALE)

(When the Nazis in Germany invaded Holland in 1940, they began to persecute all Jews. Anne Frank's father took his family into hiding in an upper room of a house. In such trouble as that Anne Frank wrote about her ideals)

It's really a wonder that I haven't dropped all my ideals because they seem so absurd and impossible to carry out. Yet, I keep them, because in spite of everything I still believe that people are really good at heart. I simply can't build up any hopes on a foundation consisting of confusion, misery, and death. I see the world gradually being turned into a wilderness, I hear the ever-approaching thunder which will destroy us too, I can feel the sufferings of millions and yet, if I look up into the heavens, I think it will all come right, that this cruelty too will end, and that peace and tranquillity will return again.

In the meantime, I must uphold my ideals, for perhaps the time will come when I shall be able to carry them out.

ADAPTED FROM 'THE DIARY OF ANNE FRANK'

BIBLE READINGS

Genesis 1.26–31	—	Made in the image of God
Psalm 8	—	What is man?
Psalm 139.13–18	—	God knows me
Proverbs 20.11	—	We are known by our actions
Micah 6.8	—	What God asks of me
Matthew 10.29–31	—	Worth more than a sparrow!

Growing up

SEE ALSO:
39a,66,72a

(*a*) When we were one
We'd just begun.
When we were three
We'd left mother's knee.
With school at five
New worlds came alive.
When we were six
We were full of tricks.
At the age of seven
We know seven times eleven.
By the time that we're eight
We've learnt to think straight.
And when we are nine
We share what is 'mine'.
So when we are ten
We are almost men.

J. & E. YOUNG
(slightly adapted)

(*b*) You are changing! You begin to change the moment you are born and you go on changing all your life. Did you know that even the cells which make up your flesh are dying all the time and new cells are being created? You don't keep the same flesh all your life; it is completely replaced several times over.

(*c*) So many things to do; so many things to learn; so many people to meet; so many days to live. Father, we thank you that we are growing up in your exciting world of discovery and surprise. *Amen.*

(*a*) Heavenly Father, you know how we look forward to growing up. Help us, though, to make the most of being young, and prepare ourselves sensibly and patiently for the time when we shall have to earn our living and be parents and teachers ourselves. As we grow in size and in years, may we also grow in our understanding of you and of your ways with us. For Jesus Christ's sake. *Amen.*

JOHN BRYANT & DAVID WINTER

(*b*) Now I'm growing up,
Year after year after year
Age steps upon me.

Haiku (Japanese poetic form). STEVEN WATSON (AGED 13)

(*c*) For the body, health;
For the mind, beauty;
For the spirit, joy.

A WELSH PRAYER

(*d*) I used to think that grown-up people chose
To have stiff backs and wrinkles round their nose,
And veins like small fat snakes on either hand,
On purpose to be grand.
Till through the banisters I watched one day
My great-aunt Etty's friend who was going away,
And how her onyx beads had come unstrung.
I saw her grope to find them as they rolled;
And then I knew that she was helplessly old,
As I was helplessly young.

FRANCES CORNFORD

(*a*) As Jesus grew up in body
and mind, he grew also
in the love of God and
of those who knew him.

Luke 2.52

(*b*) Can any of you make
himself an inch taller
however much he
worries about it?

Luke 12.25
tr. J. B. PHILLIPS

(*c*) He is a good lad – never given us any trouble:
Knows how to use plane and chisel,
The different feels of wood.
Since he could grasp a nail he's helped me here,
Held planks for measuring,
And watched while I fashioned yokes and ploughs.
He'll be a craftsman – he has the hands . . .

Just twelve. Next March he'll come with us
Up to Jerusalem for the Passover.
A man already – and only yesterday
I built his cradle for him. Yes, time passes.
He knows his books, the Rabbi says,
Better than he does – that's his joke, of course –
And cuts his letters in the sand
As clear as any scholar.
Friday's trumpet never bothers him,
And Sabbaths he marches to the House of Gathering
Like other boys to sport. You should see him
Sitting cross-legged among the scattered herbs
Watching the readers' mouths, to taste
The flavour of their words!
Then the Prophets: quite often he is chosen –
Mary's proud then – and reads their thoughts as his.
A ringing voice. Isaiah's his favourite.

CLIVE SAMSON

Girls –

(*a*) With the growth spurt about the age of eleven there comes a much more mature and sensible attitude to life in general. At about this time girls tend to become much more reliable and sensible. In many years as the Headmaster of a Primary School I have found the girls in my top classes to become much more responsible than the boys of the same age . . . With this maturation there also comes an increase in interest in their appearance. . . . From about the age of twelve a girl generally becomes much more conscious of her appearance. She experiments with different hair styles. She wants to get out of school uniform when she goes out. She begs and pleads for shoes with higher heels, nylons, pretty blouses and fashionable skirts . . . the growing girl is becoming increasingly aware of the male sex, and almost certainly desires to make a good impression on the boys in the neighbourhood.

This is my life/Growing up

– and boys

(*b*) As (boys) begin to change physically into young men so almost overnight does their attitude to their appearance. Many a mother has been literally astonished to find that suddenly young Jim does not need to be told, almost forced, to wash. He becomes suddenly aware of the disfiguring line of dirt which he has always worn cheerfully below his nails. He starts to train his hair in a new style, uses haircream and toothpaste and suddenly becomes concerned about the sort of trousers he wears, the design and colour of his socks and ties and shirts, and can't possibly walk down the street with a button missing from his jacket or a hole in his elbow sleeve. Yes! You've guessed it! The boy is now a young man and he wants a girl friend. He now wants to make a good impression on the girls he meets . . .

H. W. TAME

Two of the most interesting characters I have met are my little brother Georgie, aged two months and my great Grandfather aged ninety-seven years two months.

I am interested in both. To my amazement their needs are similar and yet I would have thought that Grandpa would have had fewer needs than Georgie. After all, Georgie has need to develop the habits of taking care of himself whereas Grandpa has already learned these things, yet I have heard Mummy say that Georgie is too young to eat meat and Grandpa is now too old for it.

Georgie must be treated with care and gentleness because his bones are weak through lack of age – Grandpa's bones are weak because of over age.

The house must be quiet when Georgie sleeps because he wakens so easily. Grandpa always goes early to bed and otherwise spends much of his time dozing in his rocking-chair.

Grandpa has outgrown the use of a comb and Georgie has not yet grown old enough to need one.

Georgie has not yet the need of a toothbrush. Grandpa stopped cleaning his last remaining tooth four years ago and cannot manage with the new-fangled false ones.

Georgie is quite inactive having not yet the strength or ability to walk by himself. Similarly, Grandpa is unable to walk because he has 'screws'!

Little Georgie is without understanding and wisdom, and Grandfather is past the age of having to understand – his attitude to be wise (as he was a few years ago) is now gone with his memory.

Sounds mean nothing to either of them. Grandfather cannot hear them and Georgie is not yet interested in where they come from or what they mean.

Sometimes Grandpa utters little mumbling noises to himself which mean nothing to either himself or anybody else – unless little Georgie understands them because he also does the same thing – perhaps they are talking to each other in a language of their own!

Both need warmth and are well wrapped up in shawls.

(*continued*)

Grandpa sucks his pipe while little Georgie sucks his thumb.

Perhaps this is what the adults mean when they say, 'He is a chip off the old block!' Oh, I forgot to tell you that Grandpa's name is George!

LYNN BOTTOMLEY (AGED 10)

(*a*) Father, we know our bodies are growing all the time. We can't stop them and we don't want to. It happens without any effort of our own will, for growth has its own secret ways. But we also know that good food, healthy exercise and restful sleep are a part of the secret. We know that feeling happy at home and school and accepting every opportunity to learn helps the secret ways of growth. Although we cannot make ourselves grow, help us to co-operate with the quiet ways of nature. *Amen.*

(*b*) For those whose bodies fail to grow properly,
For those whose minds are not fully developed,
For those who have never heard of your love,
Father, for these we pray. *Amen.*

When a male animal is old enough to produce sperms and the female to produce eggs they mate and produce young. Many animals treat their partners quite differently from human beings: they simply mate and then leave each other. That is an end to it and the young are often left to their own devices.

Man is different and that is one reason why he is called 'the highest creation'. He understands the meaning of words like 'caring' and 'responsibility' and 'love'. Babies are born as helpless creatures that need great care and attention in their early years. They are completely dependent on their parents for food, warmth and love.

This is one of the many good reasons for marriage. It is in the security and warmth of a home, cared for by parents who are old enough to do so, that a baby has the best chance of growing up in happiness. You have many steps to take before you can be ready for so great an adventure. You will have to be at school well into your teens because there is so much to learn to prepare for life in this busy modern world. You may want to go on to college or university or begin an apprenticeship; and if you get the chance, you will be wise to do so.

To marry and raise a family needs a house, furniture and a job to provide the money; and the time will come when you are able to plan all this. Your body is the first part of you to be ready to step into adult life; it must now wait with patience for the rest of you to catch up. The years of teenage are extremely important; they are preparation years.

BIBLE READINGS

1 Chronicles 28.20	—	A father's advice
Luke 2.39–40	—	Jesus grows up
Ephesians 4.11–13, 15–16	—	Growing to be like Jesus
2 Timothy 3.14–15	—	Stick to your beliefs

Curiosity and search

SEE ALSO:
9b,42a,
132b,137

Astronauts hurtle through space to explore the moon. Plans are being made to penetrate planets even further afield. On earth archaeologists carry out their 'digs', unfolding secrets of the past. Deep in the sea man discovers new wonders. The scientist peers through his microscope at things invisible to the naked eye.

The driving force behind all this ceaseless activity is – curiosity; something which has been a spur to man from the beginning of time. Each of us has his share of this urge to find things out, to make discoveries, to fill gaps in our knowledge.

Curiosity starts when we are very young. Have you seen a baby when he first discovers that he's got fingers? He holds his hands up, peers at them and wiggles his fingers to make them move. One hand touches the other as he explores what it feels like. Later, he discovers his nose, ears and hair as he explores his own body. Still later, it will be the big wide world he wants to explore. Watch him when, in his bath, he discovers what water can do!

It is because men have asked 'Why?' and 'How?' that electricity has been discovered, the car engine invented, Everest climbed, bridges built, great seas charted and the moon explored. 'Why?' and 'How?' are questions that all men, from primitive times to the twentieth century, have asked. As we find the answer to our questions, so we grow and understand the world better.

(*a*) Tree and flower and leaf and grass,
Let them pass, let them pass!
Hill and water under sky,
Pass them by, pass them by!
Still round the corner there may wait
A new road, or a secret gate . . .

J. R. TOLKIEN

(*b*) Dear God,
I'm thinking about the wind,
And about You.

I can't see the wind,
But it's very real.
I can feel the wind,
And I can see what the wind does,
Ruffling my hair,
Moving the leaves on the trees,
Blowing into the sails to carry a boat along.

Dear God,
I don't understand all about You,
But I know You are real.
I know You can touch my inside thoughts,
I know You are always there.
I can't see You,
But You are real. And You love me.

You understand all about me;
I can talk to You,
And listen to You inside my thoughts.
I'm like a small boat with a sail,
And You can move me along
To try things with You and for You,
To adventure with You and for You.

Thank You, God,
For being God. *Amen.*

LILIAN COX

(*a*) When you are studying any matter or considering any philosophy, ask yourself only what are the facts and what is the truth that the facts bear out. Never let yourself be diverted either by what you would wish to believe or by what you think would have beneficial social effects it if were believed. But look only at what are the facts.

BERTRAND RUSSELL

(*b*) The world goes ever, ever on,
Rolling along through space and time,
God ever guarding from above
While man toils up his dangerous climb.
But will he ever reach the height,
That pinnacle divine of love,
Or will he slip upon the way,
Slip downward from so far above?

I think perhaps – no, I am sure –
That there will come for us a day
When we shall reach the longed-for point,
That point for which we daily pray.
Then our life will be glorious;
Of pain and wrong there shall be none;
And man's great upwards battle won.

R. J. MAXWELL (AGED 11)

(*c*) Keep asking – it will be given you;
keep looking – you will find;
keep knocking – the door will be opened.
Everyone who keeps asking, gets;
everyone who keeps looking, finds;
to everyone who keeps knocking, the door opens.

Matthew 7.7–8 (*New World,* ALAN T. DALE)

(*a*) Then David decided that he must have a God: it might help. But which God should he choose? It was important to find the right one. If only he had listened more carefully to what the men had talked about in the camp! He had been interested only in learning new words. If he had asked more questions, he would have learnt a lot more.

What gods did he know of? The one the Jews had made so many demands to in return for his help? And what had David to give? Nothing! And if you were not a Jew, perhaps you had no right to choose him. The God of the Catholics seemed to leave things to a woman called Mary. Not that David had anything against women, but as he knew so little about them it might be better to choose one who looked after things himself. Johannes should have taught him something about God. Instead, he had only told him about a man, also called David, who had lived a long time ago. David dug into his memory: when he thought hard he could recall many of the things Johannes had said. Was not there something about a god, too, in that story about David? Something in rather difficult words – he had always liked new words that were long and strange: he enjoyed finding out what they meant.

Suddenly it came back to him. That other David had said of his God, 'He maketh me to lie down in green pastures, He leadeth me beside the still waters.'

He was the one he would choose!

ANNE HOLM

(*b*) Sun and wind and sea –
The road is wide before us –
Though dark the storms break o'er us,
We shall victors be.
For not by might or power,
But by the high decision
Of all who see the vision,
The world is free.

JOHN MORRISON

Where is God?

(*a*) In every place where you find the imprint of men's feet, there I am.
The Talmud (A Hebrew book)

(*b*) God is seated in the hearts of all.
The Bhagavad-Gita
(A Hindu book)

(*c*) Where can I go to escape you?
You are wherever I am.
If I climb the skies
or explore the underworld,
you are there!
If I fly with the sun
from dawn to dark,
your hand's still on my shoulder,
your right hand grips me!
If I say, 'I'll lose myself in the darkness,
vanish in the night!'
darkness is no darkness to you,
night is bright as day,
darkness as light!
I thank you for being what you are –
awe-inspiring, wonderful,
wonderful in all you do.
You made me the man I am
in the depth of being;
you've known what I am really like
from the moment I was born.
You have watched the marvel of my body,
the wonder of my birth;
What you think of me matters to me, O God,
more than anything else –
how much you know about me!
I cannot fathom your thoughts
any more than I can count the sand on the shore!
Yet after all my searching
I am still in your presence!

(Psalm 139.7–18) (*Winding Quest*, ALAN T. DALE)

(*a*) *Thanksgiving for the pioneers*

God, we give thanks for the pioneers of the human race, who believed that man could travel on the waters, and did not rest until they had made boats; who believed that man could travel in a horseless chariot, and laboured through difficulty and scorn until an engine was built; who believed that man could fly, and persevered until at last the air was conquered; who believed that space was open to our exploration and built rockets and capsules with great daring. We thank you for those in the world today who believe that cancer can be banished, and poverty and war abolished, and leisure and education and comfort provided freely for all mankind. Bless those bold spirits; strengthen their hearts and their arms. Save us from ever scoffing, and may we share their faith and lend our aid towards the accomplishment of the new triumphs which you have put into the dreams and hopes of mankind.
Amen.

S. G. HEDGES (altd.)

(*b*) Take ship, my soul,
Joyous launch out on trackless seas,
Fearless for unknown shores to sail,
Chanting a song pleasant of exploration.
Away, brave souls!
Farther and farther sail!
O daring joy but safe.
Are they not all the seas of God?
On farther, farther, farther sail!

WALT WHITMAN

BIBLE READINGS

Job 12.7–9	—	Creation helps us know God
Luke 2.41–51	—	Jesus asks questions
Luke 7.18–23; 9.18–22 John 1.35–42; 3.1–15	}	Curiosity about Jesus

Common senses—

To see

SEE ALSO:
79a,b,82,83,85a,b,
108a,112a,139a,b

(*a*) You promised me my life; but you lied. You think that life is nothing but not being stone dead. It is not the bread and water I fear. I can live on bread: when have I asked for more? It is no hardship to drink water if the water be clean. . . . But to shut me from the sight of the fields and flowers; to chain my feet so that I can never again ride with the soldiers nor climb the hills; to make me breathe foul damp darkness, and keep me from everything that brings me back to the love of God . . . all this is worse than the furnace in the bible that was heated seven times. I could do without my warhorse; I could drag about in a skirt; I could let the banners and the trumpets and the knights and soldiers pass me and leave me behind as they leave the other women, if only I could still hear the wind in the trees, the larks in the sunshine, the young lambs crying through the healthy frost, and the blessed blessed church bells that send my angel voices floating to me on the wind. But without these things I cannot live. . . .

From *St. Joan* by GEORGE BERNARD SHAW

(*St. Joan was to be burnt at the stake as a heretic but she recanted and so was saved, only to be told she would be imprisoned for life. The speech above shows the kind of answer she gave*).

(*a*) FARTHEST VISIBLE OBJECT: The remotest heavenly body clearly visible with the naked eye is the Great Galaxy in *Andromeda* (Mag. 3.47). This is a rotating nebula in spiral form, and its distance from the Earth is about 2,200,000 light years or about 13,000,000,000,000,000,000 miles (21 x 10^{18}km). It is just possible, however, that, under ideal seeing conditions, Messier 33, the Spiral in Triangulum (Mag. 5.79), can be glimpsed by the naked eye of keen-sighted people at a distance of 2,300,000 light years.

From *Guinness Book of Records*

(*b*) EARLIEST TV SERVICE: The world's first high definition (i.e. 405 lines) television broadcasting service was opened from Alexandra Palace, London, N.22, on 2 Nov. 1936, when there were about 100 sets in the United Kingdom. The Chief Engineer was Mr. Douglas Birkinshaw. A television station in Berlin, Germany, made a low definition (180 lines) transmission from 22 March 1935. The transmitter burnt out in Aug. 1935.

From *Guinness Book of Records*

(*c*) See what a lovely shell,
Small and pure as a pearl,
Lying close to my foot,
Frail, but a work divine,
Made so fairily well
With delicate spire and whorl,
How exquisitely minute –
A miracle of design!

What is it? A learned man
Could give it a clumsy name.
Let him name it who can –
The beauty would be the same.

ALFRED, LORD TENNYSON

(*a*) Why should I envy what money can buy
As long as a blackbird sings?
As long as a peacock butterfly
Will open its gaudy wings?

Why should I envy the world at large
As long as the sun flings gems
In the wake of any passing barge
That glides on a silver Thames?

As long as I see in the summer sky,
Unnoticed by the crowds,
The greatest show on earth float by,
The fleets of sailing clouds?

Have never a fear it will come to pass
That I envy a millionaire,
While dew on a tuft of scrubby grass
Can flash like a solitaire.

DERMOT MCKAY

(*b*) CAMERAS: The earliest photograph was taken in the summer of 1826 by Joseph Nicéphore Niépce (1765–1833), a French physician and scientist. It showed the courtyard of his country house at Gras, near St. Loup-de-Varennes. It probably took eight hours to expose and was taken on a bitumen coated polished pewter plate measuring 7¾ in. by 6½ in. (20 × 16.5cm.). The earliest photograph taken in England was one of a diamond-paned window in Laycock (or Lacock) Abbey, Wiltshire, taken in August 1835 by William Henry Fox Talbot, MP (1800–77), the inventor of the negative-positive process. This was bought by the Johannesburg City Council for £480 in November 1970. The world's first aerial photograph was taken in 1858 by Gaspard Félix Tournachon (1820–1910), alias Nadar, from a balloon near Villacoublay, on the outskirts of Paris, France.

From *Guinness Book of Records*

(*a*) Our eyes work in the same way as a camera. At the back of our eyes is a sensitive part called the retina which can be compared to the film. As it receives images from outside light it sends messages along nerves to the brain reporting what it is receiving from outside objects. The light enters the eye through a lens which is surrounded by muscles which alter its shape thus allowing it to focus on objects at different distances.

(*b*) I am now about to close my eyelids, Lord,
For my eyes this evening have finished their work
And will return home,
Having walked for a day in the garden of men.
Thank you, Lord, for my eyes, windows open on the wide world;
Thank you for their look that carries my soul as the broad sunbeam carries the light and warmth of your sun.
I pray to you during the night, that, tomorrow, when I open my eyes to the clear morning,
They shall be ready to serve both my soul and my God.
May my eyes be clear and straightforward, Lord, and give others a hunger for purity;
May my look never be one of disappointment,
disillusionment,
despair;
But may it know how to admire,
contemplate,
adore.
May my eyes learn to close in order to find you more easily;
But may they never turn away from the world because they are afraid.
May my eyes be penetrating enough to recognize your presence in the world,
And may they never shut on the afflictions of men.

MICHEL QUOIST

(*a*) Look upon the rainbow, and praise him that made it;
Very beautiful it is in the brightness thereof.
It compasseth the heavens about with a glorious circle,
And the hands of the most High have bended it.

ECCLESIASTICUS 43.11,12

(*b*) I saw the fog grow thick,
Which soon made blind my ken;
It made tall men of boys,
And giants of tall men.

It clutched my throat, I coughed;
Nothing was in my head
Except two heavy eyes
Like balls of burning lead.

And when it grew so black
That I could know no place,
I lost all judgement then,
Of distance and of space.

The street lamps, and the lights
Upon the halted cars,
Could either be on earth
Or be the heavenly stars.

A man passed by me close,
I asked my way, he said,
'Come, follow me, my friend' –
I followed where he led

He rapped the stones in front,
'Trust me,' he said, 'and come';
I followed like a child –
A blind man led me home.

W. H. DAVIES

To hear

(*a*) Be quiet now.
Birds are singing,
Bells are ringing,
Postmen knocking,
Listen hard.

Be still now.
Rain is dripping,
Wind is blowing,
Car doors slamming,
Listen hard.

Be silent now.
Planes are flying,
Ships are hooting,
Dockers working,
Listen hard.

Be hushed now.
Cows are mooing,
Sheep are bleating,
Tractor chugging,
Listen hard.

Be gentle now.
Doves are cooing,
Babes are crying,
People sighing,
Listen hard.

(*b*) The ear is a very delicate piece of mechanism. First there is the drum, which waves of sound coming through the air cause to vibrate. These vibrations cause a little chain of bones to move. The bones are hinged together and so tiny that they are about the size of half a grain of barley. The third one of these bones touches a membrane stretched across a cavity which is filled with fluid, and its movement causes waves in this fluid. These waves agitate some tiny endings of nerves causing electric impulses to pass along the eighth cranial nerve to the auditory centre of the brain and the person so stimulated says, 'I hear.'

T. H. SUTCLIFFE

(*c*) After talking to the people and telling them parables and other stories Jesus often used to add these words:
"Listen, then, if you have ears to hear with!"

Playground sounds

(*a*) The leaves are rustling themselves in the trees and the trees are moving, groaning heavy sound. The twigs are crackling, snapping and spluttering. They crackle and pop when you crunch them with your foot. The children scuffle and shuffle across the playground. They kick stones with a scrubbing sound. You can hear an engine in the lane whining, whizzing down the bank. I can hear the children's voices talking. They sometimes make the birds twitter but the chattering birds have gone away today. It is winter. There is silence.

JOHN (AGED 9)

Factory Noises

(*b*) At first it was deafening. You couldn't hear a thing if anybody spoke to you. There were black oily machines everywhere spinning their drills like silver needles churning out the blue metal in long winding coils all over the floor which was like thick black mud. You had to mind you didn't slip. A bit further down there were some men welding with masks on like men from outer space. They had torches shooting blue flames which you could not look at because they might blind you. There was a terribly choking smell coming from these welding torches and I could taste it in my mouth a long time after we got back to school. Every time a man finished a job he threw a piece of metal into an iron box and this made a deafening clang! We only stayed in there a few minutes and we were not allowed to go close but it was enough for me. I never want to go there again.

GAIL (AGED 10)

(*a*) The wren's sweet song;
The cuckoo's cry;
Larks singing
In the clear blue sky;
My dog's gay bark;
Wind in the wheat
On golden days
Of summer heat;
The babbling murmur
Of a stream
Over the stones,
Coolly a-gleam;
The hum of insects;
Robin's call
When autumn leaves
Begin to fall;
Sparrows' lively
Chirruping
When crumbs to them
Each day I fling;
The zoom of bees
In lazy flight –
These sounds to me
Bring rich delight!

MALCOLM HEMPHREY

(*b*) Bubbling water,
Bubbling stream,
Howling wind,
Hissing stream.

Crackling wood,
Clanking chain,
Pealing bells,
Pattering rain.

Noises, noises,
All around,
Listen! Listen!
Can you hear a sound?

JOAN SABIN

(*c*) Sound travels at a definite speed. The speed of sound is 1,100 feet per second. This is equivalent to 750 miles an hour. If an aeroplane travels faster than sound it 'breaks the sound barrier' which, for a long time, scientists thought was quite impossible. Then the air around the nose of the plane becomes highly compressed and makes a shock wave which reaches the earth as a loud bang.

Thank you, God, for this wonderful world,
for all its sights and sounds
that please us.

Thank you for the sounds of human voices:

Whispering, speaking out loud,
shouting, singing,
giving expression to sorrow and joy,
to prayer and praise;
teaching, amusing,
encouraging and guiding.

Thank you for the sounds of human labour:

Turning wheels, banging hammers,
roaring engines, ringing bells,
whining sirens, clacking typewriters
and rattling pots and pans.

Thank you for the sounds of nature:

Birds singing,
sea-gulls calling,
dogs barking, cats miaowing,
cows mooing, horses neighing;
the sea's roar,
the rain's pour,
the wind's whistle,
the stream's ripple.

Thank you God for these
and all the sounds
that please us.
Thank you, God,
for the sounds of silence.

ALAN GAUNT

To taste

(*a*) Hot enough to startle the tongue, its sweetness meets my mouth's dryness. Well-stirred, its liveliness wakens my body. Now I can move! I am myself again! The taste grows stronger, gaining power. One leg, then another; I am out of bed, alive! The early morning cup of tea has dragged me from my sleep. Welcome morning!

(*b*) A raw carrot you get from the garden is scrumptious, munchious and delicious. You can break it off with a snap, and pop a bit in your mouth to crunch up and chew and when you chew it it tastes sweet and juicy, cold and crisp in your mouth. Then you hold it tight and bite into it with a terrific crack! You can feel great chunks of it being ground up by your teeth and every chew is mouth-watering and sweet. It is a rich and juicy thing; a carrot is like free ice cream.

RAYMOND (AGED 10)

(*c*) We struck a spring such as no one in this area had ever seen before – nearly three feet in diameter and coming with enough force to toss a man into the air. . . . It was an eighth wonder of the world for a time and a real problem was to get the water level low enough to allow the men to build. Our drought had not yet broken, and as Raja Reddy pumped out this abundance of cool sweet water and saw it run to waste across the fields he had to suffer with the knowledge that 30 miles away in his own fruit gardens all the wells were dry and his trees were dying at the rate of 50 a day. . . . On October 7th we had a service of thanksgiving for water. The valves were opened and water came out of the taps! I had never felt before the miracle of water – cool, sweet water.

A LETTER FROM S. INDIA

To smell

(*a*) Why is it that the poets tell
So little of the sense of smell?
These are the odours I love well:

The smell of coffee, freshly ground;
Or rich plum pudding, holly-crowned;
Or onions fried and deeply browned.

The fragrance of a fumy pipe;
The smell of apples, newly ripe;
And printers' ink on leaden type.

Woods by moonlight in September
Breathe most sweet; and I remember
Many a smoky camp-fire ember.

Camphor, turpentine, and tea,
The balsam of a Christmas tree,
These are the whiffs of gramarye –
A ship smells best of all to me!

CHRISTOPHER MORLEY

(*b*) I like the smell of new-sawn wood.
I love the smell of tar!
I think I like that leath'ry smell
You get in a brand new car.

I like the smell of burning leaves,
And roses after rain.
I like . . . oh, yes! that lilac tree
Smells lovely down the lane.

I like the smell of oranges,
And pears and peaches too,
And fresh-baked cakes and toasting bread
And ev'ry kind of stew!

The smell of scented soap is nice.
And then – now, let me see!
Well! Now I've had my bath tonight,
I like the smell of me!

F. ROGERSON

To touch

(*a*) I often run the sole of my bare foot
along the cat's back,
Velvet, warm and soft.
Silk is glorious to touch and rub:
Soft, shiny paper.
Lush grass is nice to run over.
Milk tops are sensational to rub.
The rubber underside of a ground-sheet:
Worn, shiny wood.
Slippery tiles,
Also smooth stones are beautiful
to touch, and
Metal and
Canvas, lovely rough canvas.

STEPHEN TAYLOR (9 YEARS)

(*b*) For the feel of warm wool, soft to the skin,
And the polished touch of smooth wood.
We praise and thank the Creator of all things.

For the gentle stroke of cats' fur,
And the touch of a hamster's coat,
We praise and thank the Creator of all things.

For the bite of cold snow, hard-pressed into a ball,
And the trickle of sand through the fingers,
We praise and thank the Creator of all things.

When I see a salmon leap the fall,
or the aer'plane's silver trail –
or a drop of water magnified,
then my eyes and soul bless the Lord.

When I hear the frosty crunch of snow,
or the sun-drenched hum of the bee,
or a well-tuned engine whine with power,
then my ears and soul bless the Lord.

After rain the smell of clean fresh air
blows soft and cool and free;
when the strawberries are turned to jam,
then my nose and soul bless the Lord.

At the taste of berries gathered free,
or the tang of sea food, mint or treacle,
touch of velvet, feel of cold smooth stones;
hands and tongue and soul bless the Lord.

GRACIE KING

BIBLE READINGS

Job 12.11	—	Hearing and taste
Proverbs 20.12	—	Ear and eye
Luke 6.39–42	—	A different kind of blindness
Luke 18.35–43	—	Sight restored
1 Corinthians 12.14–26	—	The harmony of the body

Learning

SEE ALSO:
10a,13c,15c,21a,
69,70a,72a,b,c,142a,b,c,
143c

(*a*) For the first years of your life you rely on grown-ups, who know all that happens or does not happen in the world, what you must do and when and how you must do it. Then youth comes. Everything in the world turns out to be inconstant and changing, and not always reasonable. You begin to notice that grown-ups are not as reliable as all that; they often make mistakes, and hesitate, and disagree with one another, sometimes even contradict themselves, and do not know nearly all there is to know. Now you often have to do things on your own initiative and at your own risk. Roads divide, and at each cross-roads you are faced with the difficult problem of choosing your own path. You have already gathered a certain experience of life, and are impatient and hungry for more.

SAMUEL MARSHAK

(*b*) Give me today, O God, the mind which can really learn.
Give me
the attentive mind, that I may concentrate all
the time on what I am hearing and doing;
the retentive mind, that I may not hear and forget,
but that I may grasp a thing and remember it;
the open mind, that no prejudice may blind me to
truth I do not wish to see;
the eager mind, that I may not be content to remain
as I am, but that every day I may try to add
something new to my store of knowledge and of skill,
and something finer to my store of goodness.
This I ask for Jesus' sake. *Amen.*

WILLIAM BARCLAY

(*a*) Turn on the television, soon we shall see
Pictures of people, great mountains, the sea,
Far distant countries, small insects, new sights,
Folk telling stories with laughter and fright.
Thank you, our Father, wherever we turn,
There are people to help us discover and learn.

Books in the bookcase just wait to be read,
Curled up in a chair or lying in bed,
Some tell us a story or delve in the past;
Others teach us new words, explain truths that will last.
Thank you, our Father, wherever we turn,
There are people to help us discover and learn.

Five days a week off to school we all go,
We don't miss a day; there's so much to know:
To write and to read, learn maths and to paint,
So open the book, find the page, what's the date?
Thank you, our Father, wherever we turn,
There are people to help us discover and learn.

Then, when it's Sunday, we all come together,
Babies and parents, sisters and brothers,
Minister, teachers and friends in the pew,
For hymns, stories, pictures; some old, others new.
Thank you, our Father, wherever we turn,
There are people to help us discover and learn.

(*b*) A book is a teaching machine. It is composed of the finest printed circuits, but it is completely non-electric. It has been produced in its present form for more than 500 years, and is still man's most successful device for bridging space to connect one thoughtful mind with another.

AN AMERICAN PUBLISHER'S ADVERTISEMENT

(*a*) So Andrew Carnegie had resolved then that if ever wealth came to him, he would try to give many millions what he himself had been lucky enough to have. Books! These were what he wanted to be remembered for. Today his name stands large on some 2,811 libraries in the USA, Britain and other English-speaking countries. When he had retired from business in 1901 and sold all his shares and other property, he was said to be worth as much as 500 million dollars – then worth over 100 million pounds. After he had initiated his huge library scheme, there was money enough still for other endowments. So we find today Carnegie universities, colleges of all kinds, art galleries, scholarships, craft schools, musical centres – and in his own home town of Dunfermline a public park, among many other endowments. He was anxious that all his benefactions might help mankind not just for the moment, but in perpetuity. Today the Carnegie Foundation in America continues his work and the administration of the funds he left.

VERA BURTT

(*b*) Asked how it felt to be able at last to read, an elderly man replied that he had never felt so hungry in his life. He didn't mean bodily hunger. He had learned to read, only to find that in his language there were hardly any books. Another man whose son had taught him to read said, "Give me all the books you have in my language". There were just three. Few of us ever stop to think what we should do without books. We take for granted the daily newspaper, the weekly and monthly magazine, the books in the library or on our own shelves and we forget the millions of people in the world who, having learned to read, find it so difficult to obtain reading material.

From a *Feed the Minds* circular.

(*a*) The family settled in Allegheny, Pennsylvania; a primitive place with no railway to anywhere, just a river steamer. Andrew Carnegie hated his first job as a bobbin boy in a cotton factory. Soon, he fixed himself up with a better job – as a messenger boy to the telegraph company. And now he put his foot on the ladder that was to lead him to a remarkable career. He knew that if he learnt the Morse Code he could get a much better job – so he taught himself Morse. This intense desire to 'know more' was symbolic of his whole life. He never stopped learning . . .

VERA BURTT

(*b*) By the end of the working day most piecers were too tired to play, and certainly in no frame of mind to learn. David Livingstone and a handful of other children were made of sterner stuff. Defying aching limbs and tired minds, they made their way to the company school to spend two hours, from 8 to 10 p.m., learning to read and write. . . . Already taught to read and write by his father, Livingstone started Latin during his first year of evening school. During the next few years he spent what little money he did not give to his mother on classical textbooks. At night he often read till midnight, his mother frequently having to take his book away before he would go to sleep. Six hours later he would be in the mills again.

TIM JEAL

BIBLE READINGS

Job 28.12–28	—	Where is wisdom?
Proverbs 1.1–6, 8–9	—	True understanding
Acts 8.26–39	—	Seizing an opportunity
2 Timothy 2.1–2	—	Teachers and writings
Wisdom of Solomon 6.12–21 (Apocrypha)	—	In praise of wisdom

Feelings

SEE ALSO:

12,58,60,
61a,b,62a,
64,88a,121b

(*a*) LOVE

Longing to share
Longing to care
seeking
in pain – in despair
the brother
in
the
OTHER

ALICE A. GORGE

Joy

(*b*)

Bursting into life
With an earthquake's force,
Just like fireworks tossed
Comes joy!

Beat it on the drum,
Like the thunder's roar,
Let the storm outpour
Our joy!

Swing the clarinet
Into sparkling song,
And we'll march along
With joy!

Plucking the guitar
To a throbbing beat,
We will tap the feet
With joy!

As the organ chords
Add their melody,
We'll make our choice
In joy!

And the Son of Man
Gives to all their lead,
It's just what we need
For joy!

So we join as one
Giving Him the praise
For these glad new days
Of joy!

Let the whole world swing
And the cosmos ring,
As we celebrate
Our joy!

VALERIE M. DUNN

Hope

(*a*) I have a dream that one day this nation will rise up and live out the true meaning of its creed. "We hold these truths to be self-evident: that all men are created equal."

I have a dream that one day on the red hills of Georgia the sons of former slaves and the sons of former slave-owners will be able to sit down together at the table of brotherhood. I have a dream that my four little children will one day live in a nation where they will not be judged by the colour of their skin, but by the content of their character. I have a dream today.

I have a dream that one day down in Alabama . . . little black boys and black girls will be able to join hands with little white boys and white girls as sisters and brothers. I have a dream . . .

This is our hope. This is the faith that I go back to the south with. With this faith we will be able to hew out of the mountain of despair a stone of hope.

Extracts from a speech by Dr. Martin Luther King, an American negro minister who believed in tolerance between black and white people and was assassinated on April 4th, 1968.

Happiness

(*b*) Happiness is a
fragile bubble;
Forget yourself, its
size will double.
But selfish greed
and lustful thirst
will only make
your bubble burst.

PETER TONGEMAN

Effort (by the first man to run a mile in 4 minutes)

(*a*) I had a moment of mixed joy and anguish, when my mind took over. It raced well ahead of my body and drew my body compellingly forward. I felt that the moment of a lifetime had come. There was no pain, only a great unity of movement and aim. The world seemed to stand still, or did not exist.

I felt at that moment that it was my chance to do one thing supremely well. I drove on, impelled by a combination of fear and pride.

Those last few seconds seemed never-ending. The faint line of the finishing tape stood ahead as a haven of peace, after the struggle. The arms of the world were waiting to receive me if only I reached the tape without slackening my speed. I leapt at the tape like a man taking his last spring to save himself from the chasm that threatens to engulf him.

My effort was over and I collapsed almost unconscious with an arm on either side of me.

ROGER BANNISTER

Fear

(*b*) High up in a tree swaying in the wind,
I sat myself on a thick green rotten branch,
Where long since the insects made their home,
And on the north side of the branch was damp green moss,
Which was glittering with the early morning dew;
Suddenly I lurched forward. I felt nothing but fear,
For I was falling, and from the corner of my eye I saw dark figures pass me by,
Desperately I reached out for a hold;
My hands grasped gratefully for a friendly branch
To halt my nightmare fall;
Then I climbed down the old gnarled tree,
Which nearly brought me grief.

ROY SEAMAN (AGED 13)
Lakenham Secondary School, Norwich

Love

(*a*) Love is a great thing,
Yea, a great and thorough good;
For it carries a burden that is no burden,
And makes everything that is bitter, sweet and savoury.
Nothing is sweeter than love,
Nothing more courageous,
Nothing fuller or better in heaven and earth;
Because love is born of God.
He that loveth, flieth, runneth and rejoiceth,
He is free, and cannot be held in.

Love feels no burden, thinks nothing of trouble,
Attempts what is above its strength,
Thinks nothing impossible.
Though weary, love is not tired;
Though alarmed, it is not confounded:
But as a lively flame and burning torch,
It forces its way upwards,
And securely passes through all.

THOMAS à. KEMPIS

Hatred and forgiveness

(*b*)
I quarrelled with my brother,
I don't know what about,
One thing led to another
And somehow we fell out.
The start of it was slight,
The end of it was strong,
He said he was right,
I knew he was wrong!

We hated one another.
The afternoon turned black.
Then suddenly my brother
Thumped me on the back,
And said, 'Oh come along!
We can't go on all night –
I was in the wrong.'
So he was in the right.

ELEANOR FARJEON

(*a*) A man whose clothes were on fire staggered from an alley shouting for help and was ignored by people in the street until a coloured man took off his jacket and smothered the flames, the Newcastle upon Tyne deputy coroner, Mr. Wilfred-Kilner, was told at an inquest yesterday.

Mr. George Charles Browning, aged 63, of West Parade, Newcastle, was set alight when he and two workmates were caught in a spray of burning oil from a switch at an electricity sub-station in Fourth Lane, Newcastle, on July 28. The jury returned a verdict of Accidental Death on Percy Redhead, aged 64, of Talbot Green, Newcastle, and Joseph Gibbons, aged 62, of Chicken Road, Wallsend, both electrical fitter's mates, who died from burns and shock.

Police-Sergeant Matthew Rowley said Mr. Browning was still in hospital. He had said that there was a big flash and a muffled explosion:

'Joe and Percy were lying there, but I couldn't do anything for them because I was myself in flames. I managed to get to Westgate Road, burning and yelling for help to a lot of people, but everybody ignored me. It was a coloured man, I think a Pakistani, who took off his jacket and put the flames out.

SOURCE UNKNOWN

(*b*) Courage is like a lion
Inside you.
It is asleep –
And when you are angry
It awakes,
And you are filled,
From head to toe,
With courage.

PETER HOLLINGSWORTH (AGED 12)
Lakenham Secondary School, Norwich

Contentment

I remember listening to "Children's Hour" one afternoon in the 'thirties. Aunt Muriel told a story about an old woman who was living in a bottle and she couldn't get out, until one day, a little fairy happened to be passing by and heard the little woman's voice calling out: "Get me out from this bottle, please." Then the fairy got the old lady from the bottle.

"Thank you from the bottom of my heart, I am most grateful to you, dear." Then the fairy said: "I shall make a little house for you to live in."

The fairy waved her magic wand and, quick as a flash, the old bottle changed into a lovely white-washed cottage. The old lady was very delighted with her new home, then the fairy said: "I will come and visit you every week, my dear, and if there is anything you need, just ask me."

But every time the fairy came to visit her, the old woman always wanted something. In the end, the fairy was so annoyed with her wants, that she turned the cottage back into the old bottle again.

I thought that the story had a very good moral to it because no matter what you may give to people, they are never satisfied. They want the moon.

BILL HOWE

Bill Howe is a severely disabled spastic. "Crossed Wires" is a 40-page booklet published by the Spastics Society which took him 5 years to write. Each letter was typed with a peg fastened to his shoe on his left foot – his only limb with controllable movement.

(*a*) The June grass, amongst which I stood, was taller than I was, and I wept. I had never been so close to grass before. It towered above me and all around me, each blade tattooed with tiger-skins of sunlight. It was knife-edged, dark, and a wicked green, thick as a forest and alive with grasshoppers that chirped and chattered and leapt through the air like monkeys.

I was lost and didn't know where to move. A tropic heat oozed up from the ground, rank with sharp odours of roots and nettles. Snow-clouds of elder-blossom banked in the sky, showering upon me the fumes and flakes of their sweet and giddy suffocation. High overhead ran frenzied larks, screaming, as though the sky were tearing apart.

For the first time in my life I was out of sight of humans. For the first time in my life I was alone in a world whose behaviour I could neither predict nor fathom: a world of birds that squeeled, of plants that stank, of insects that sprang about without warning. I was lost and I did not expect to be found again.

LAURIE LEE

(*b*) On the bridge.

I asked
If you were lonely.

I like to be alone
You said.

Yet we stood
On the bridge
Talking
Till the morning.

I. CHOONARA
South Africa

Shame

He was whistling again early today.
How can an old roadsweeper be so gay?
I've got a cleaner job. And better pay.
  Yet I'm always grumbling!

She is always cheerful. Her husband died
A year ago. Three children to provide
For too. I have a partner by my side.
  Yet I'm always grumbling!

They haven't been away for years, they said.
A holiday would put them in the red.
But they're content. Soon I'm off to the 'Med'.
  Yet I'm always grumbling!

Feeding poor sparrows on her window sill,
That lonely pensioner is thankful still
For crumbs. For me, I always eat my fill.
  Yet I'm always grumbling!

The pure content of those who have so little makes me humble.
Lord, grant that I who have so much may cease to grumble.

PETER TONGEMAN

BIBLE READINGS

1 Chronicles 29.10–13 and 2 Chronicles 6.18–21	}	Awe
Job 42.1–6 and Matthew 18.1–4	}	Humility
Psalm 126	—	Joy
Psalm 137.1–4	—	Disappointment
Matthew 21.6–11	—	Excitement
Mark 14.66–72	—	Shame
James 1.26–27; 3.1–5	—	Controlling the tongue

FAMILY AND FRIENDS

THEME COMMENT

We do not and cannot live in isolation. We become our true selves only in relationship with others. "Christian Education . . . must be concerned with the whole lives of the individuals with whom it deals; and because those lives are not individual only but also social, it is concerned with them in their relationships."

(*The Family Church*, H. A. HAMILTON)

Friendship is important, therefore, not only because it is a satisfying experience in itself but also because it is crucial to our personal growth and development.

The family is our starting-point; it is there we discover the need to create relationships and test their flexibility. The first days at school impose fresh burdens and further opportunities. In prompting us to call God, 'Father', Jesus not only grants us insights into the character of God but also enriches our view of family relationships. To speak of the church as a 'family' draws on the same lively images and to extend the concept to nation and world presents a vision that has both challenged and frustrated mankind.

The formula 'the experience of a good father leads to a strong belief in God' is clearly naive but it is the experience of friendship at home and school which provides a child with the raw material of his theology. Any notion of the forgiveness of God for example, could only emerge with great difficulty unless he had learned to handle the experience of forgiveness in the less demanding surroundings of home and school.

Home

SEE ALSO: 71a,78a

(*a*) When the sun sinks, when the wind stings,
dark shadows creeping,
Then I think of home. It is safe there,
it is warm at home.

When I'm friendless, when I'm lonely,
strange faces round me,
then I think of home – of my family,
of their love that's warm.

When I do wrong, parents scold me.
If no one bothered,
what if no one cared? Warm their anger,
warm their words of love.

Loving Father, how can we thank thee?
I don't know what I'd do without a
home; Lord, we find thee
in the warmth of home.

GRACIE KING

(*b*) Men and women become friends long before they think of having children. They talk together and go out with each other to see whether they can build a happy home and enjoy each other's company for the rest of their lives. Once they are married they make sure that a safe and happy home is ready for the baby. In their marriage service they will probably have made a promise to love and look after each other, 'for better, for worse; for richer, for poorer; in sickness and in health . . . till death us do part'. It is a very serious promise to make to each other and it is one of the important differences between human beings and the majority of the rest of living things. If you asked a man and his wife to explain this difference, they would probably tell you that it is because they love each other. Their love makes them want to have children and to create a happy home for themselves and their family.

(*a*) Home is the place where you feel safe. When life is tough outside you can close the door and ignore it for a time. Then, later, you feel strong enough to try again.

Home is the place where you relax; comfy beds, easy chairs, food enough and cooked the way you like it. You recognise your own books, clothes and possessions.

Home is the place where you feel wanted. Tempers dissolve, cross words are put to one side. No matter what's happened, you won't be turned away.

Home is the place where you learn. Learn forgiveness and being with other people – laughing, arguing, scrapping, reading, talking, listening, working. Learning to live.

Home is the place you one day leave to find a partner and make another home. . . .

A house Jesus might have known

(*b*) The poor houses were like boxes, flat roofed, made perhaps of rough rafters with branches laid across and plastered with mud. This could be removed easily (see Mark 2.4). The flat roof after rain was smoothed with a stone roller, which is still done today. The roof, surrounded by a parapet, was a useful adjunct to the house for drying vegetables, ripening fruit, sleeping and saying one's prayers.

PHYLLIS DOYLE

BIBLE READINGS

2 Kings 4.8–10	}	Hospitality
Luke 10.38–42	}	Hospitality
Hebrews 13.1–2	}	Hospitality
Luke 2.51–52	—	Jesus' early home-life
Luke 8.19–21	—	A new kind of family?
2 Timothy 1.3–5	—	The influence of home

Food

SEE ALSO:
35a,b,c,105b,
110a,111a,125a,
140a,173b,175a,b

(*a*) Be gentle
When you
Touch bread.
Let it not lie
Uncared for,
Unwanted;
So often bread
Is taken for granted.
There is such beauty
In bread.
Beauty of sun and soil,
Beauty of patient toil,
Wind and rain have caressed it.
Christ often blessed it.
Be gentle
When you touch bread.

ANON

The Supermarket

(*b*) Find a trolley, push it straight,
Down the supermarket rows,
Currants, raisins, greens and meat,
That's the way the money goes!

Cornflakes in their packets tall,
Made from wheat grown on the farm;
Sugar, grapefruit, rice and tea,
Brought in ships from lands afar.

Cabbage, carrots, beans or sprouts,
Pints of milk, a jar of cream,
Lorries bring them from the farm,
Where the fields are fresh and green.

Find a trolley, push it straight,
Down the supermarket rows,
Praise to God who shows his love,
By the food the farmer grows.

(*a*) Probable country of origin: Afghanistan. Part of plant most often consumed: the root, which can be cylindrical, long and tapering, or sometimes stubby and round. Colour: can be red, white, or purple, but the cultivated variety we eat is generally a lively orange. It has been used medicinally and occasionally is dried and ground as a coffee substitute. Wines and spirits can be made from this root and it can be used in place of malt in the making of beer. It can be eaten raw or cooked, in salads, soups, stews, pies, puddings, jams. . . . This paragon among vegetables? The carrot.

SKEFFINGTON ARDRON

Turkish Delight

(*b*) I love the feel of it,
I love the taste of it.
It is my favourite sweet.

I think of Sultans who
Would eat it till they grew.
Their movements were quite slow.

My mother used to make,
At Christmas, Christmas cake,
But also she would take

A secret recipe
Till we delightedly
Were Turkish until tea.

ELIZABETH JENNINGS

(*a*) Salt, mustard, vinegar, pepper,
French almond rock,
Bread and butter for your supper
That's all mother's got.
Fish and chips and coca-cola,
Put them in a pan,
Irish stew and ice-cream soda,
We'll eat all we can.

Salt, mustard, vinegar, pepper,
French almond rock,
Bread and butter for your supper
That's all mother's got.
Egg and bacon, salted herring,
Put them in a pot,
Pickled onions, apple pudding,
We will eat the lot.

TRADITIONAL

(*b*) Father God, when you thought about making food for us, it was a marvellous idea. Thank you for good solid food like roast beef and Yorkshire, for start-the-day-right food like cornflakes or bacon, for fun foods like ice-cream and chocolate and thirst-quenching drinks like orange squash or a cup of tea. For good tasting food, body-building food, protein and vitamin, we thank you, God our Father.

BIBLE READINGS

Genesis 1.11–13	—	Plants created
Deuteronomy 26.1–4	—	Harvest thanks
Psalm 8	—	Creation is for man
Psalm 65.11–13; 104.14–15; 145.15–16; 147.8	—	Various foods
Matthew 6.11	—	Our daily bread

Friendship

SEE ALSO:
43a,46a,b,
53a,b,118b,163b,
166,167a,168,169b

Love is a special way of feeling. . . . It is the safe way we feel when we sit on our mother's lap with her arms around us tight and close.

It is the good way we feel when we talk to someone and they want to listen and don't tell us to go away and be quiet.

It is the happy way we feel when we save a bird that has been hurt . . . or feed a lost cat . . . or calm a frightened colt.

Love is found in unexpected places. . . . It is there in the quiet moment when we first discover a beautiful thing . . . when we watch a bird soar high against a pale blue sky . . . when we see a lovely flower that no one else has noticed . . . when we find a place that shelters us and is all our very own.

Love starts in little ways. . . . It may begin the day we first share our thoughts with someone else . . . or help someone who needs us. . . . Or, sometimes, it begins because, even without words, we understand how someone feels.

JOAN WALSH ANGLUND

(*a*) Once, on the rocks off Rhy Arisaig, I picked up a brown seal pup no more than a day or so old – he had the soft white baby coat more often shed in the womb, and he seemed for all the world like a toy designed to please a child. He was warm and tubby and not only unafraid but squirmingly affectionate, and I set him down again with some reluctance. But he was not to be so easily left, for as I moved off he came shuffling and humping along at my heels. After a few minutes of trying to shake him off I tried dodging and hiding behind rocks, but he discovered me with amazing agility. Finally I scrambled down to the boat and rowed quickly away, but after twenty yards he was there beside me nuzzling an oar. I was in desperation to know what to do with this unexpected foundling whose frantic mother was now snorting twenty yards away, when suddenly he responded to one of her calls and the two went off together, the pup no doubt to receive the lecture of his life.

GAVIN MAXWELL

(*b*) Whenever the dog saw David, it would wag its tail, and it went to sleep with him every night. David gradually began to grow fond of it. One evening as he lay awake wondering if the winter would ever come to an end, he held his hand out to the dog when it came to lie down beside him. He did it without thinking. Perhaps he had missed it and wanted it to come and share its warmth with him. He found himself touching its head, feeling the roundness of its skull under his hand and liking the firm warm feel of it. The dog did not move, and David let his hand glide slowly over the dog's thick coat, just once.

Then he took his hand away and lay still again. The dog lifted its head and turned towards him, and David felt its warm wet tongue carefully licking his hand. And so David and the dog became friends.

ANNE HOLM

A friend is someone who likes you. It can be a boy . . . or a cat . . . or a dog . . . or even a white mouse.

A tree can be a different kind of friend. It doesn't talk to you, but you know it likes you because it gives you apples . . . or pears . . . or cherries . . . or, sometimes, a place to swing.

A brook can be a friend in a special way. It talks to you with splashy gurgles. It cools your toes and lets you sit quietly beside it when you don't feel like speaking.

The wind can be a friend too. It sings soft songs to you at night when you are sleepy and feeling lonely. Sometimes it calls to you to play. It pushes you from behind as you walk and makes the leaves dance for you. It is always with you wherever you go, and that's how you know it likes you.

JOAN WALSH ANGLUND

BIBLE READINGS

Ruth 1.15–18	—	Ruth and Naomi
1 Samuel 18.1–5	—	David and Saul
Matthew 5.43–48	—	Love your enemies
John 15.11–17	—	Greater love has no man than this
1 Corinthians 13	—	What is love?

When things go wrong

SEE ALSO:
46b,157a,
158b,169b,
175b

(*a*) Things went wrong today, God:
You know they did,
I know they did.
Show me where it was my fault;
I'll think about that, now,
And I won't dodge or make excuses . . .

Yes God, I do see where I was wrong.
I'm sorry, dear God,
Truly sorry,
It was my fault –
Please forgive me.
Is there anything I ought to do
To put things right?
I'll think about that now, with You . . .

Yes, I see what I ought to do;
Help me, God, to do it straight away.
You will help me, I know.

And then You'll give me a new start.
Thank You, God,
Thank You for my new start. *Amen.*

LILIAN COX

(*b*) Father God,
when I'm angry with a friend,
help me to understand what (s)he is thinking;
when no one seems to care about me,
help me not to be sullen;
when I feel miserable,
remind me of the good things in life.

Amen.

(*a*) I hate being teased, God:
It's very unkind of people to tease me and laugh at me.
I'm sure You understand, and are sorry.

Are You asking me a question, God?
Are You saying, "And what about you?
Do *you* ever tease anybody, or laugh at anybody?"
I must think about that, with You . . .

I'm remembering, Lord Jesus,
That people laughed at You,
That people did worse than tease You,
They jeered at You, they mocked You,
They hurt You cruelly:
And You quietly bore it all.

You want me to copy You, Lord Jesus;
You'll help me to bear being teased,
And You'll help me never to hit back. *Amen.*

LILIAN COX

(*b*) An error confessed
May yet be blessed;
An error denied
Is multiplied.

BREMER HOFMEYR

BIBLE READINGS

Matthew 5.38–48	—	An eye for an eye?
Matthew 6.12, 14–15	}	Forgiveness
Galatians 5.26–6.2	}	Forgiveness
Hebrews 13.3	—	Prayers for prisoners

War or peace?

SEE ALSO:
46b, 120, 169b, 170b

(*a*) God grant me
Serenity to accept the things
I cannot change,
Courage to change the things
I can,
And wisdom to know the
difference.

SOURCE UNKNOWN

(*b*) Long ages ago when the world was formed, the mighty mountains cooled and crumbled into rocks and small stones. Then 'In the ultimate twinkling of an eye, far tinier than the last millimetre on a six-foot rule, there came a man. He split up the one pebble which remained of all that mountain with blows; then made an arrowhead of it, and slew his brother'.

Help us, God, to use the things you have given us in the right way, so that we can help the world to become what you want it to be.

The man could have made a tool instead of a weapon, and helped his brother to till the ground, or make useful things for his comfort.

T. H. WHITE

It was impossible to get away, for the boy was as big as himself, and to escape would mean hitting back. David shielded his head against the boy's blows and clenched his teeth. The blows began to lose some of their force, and the boy seemed to hesitate. 'So you won't hit back, eh? Scared to fight, I suppose?' David did not answer, and the boy set about him again but less violently this time – rather as if he felt he had to.

'Use your fists, you young swine!'

'No.'

The boy appeared to have grown tired of striking him, at least for the moment, and David sat up with blood streaming from his nose.

'You seem to enjoy a good hiding. Maybe you like me for giving you one!' The boy's voice was sneering. David regarded him calmly. 'No, I don't. I hate you – and I'd hate you just as much if it had been anyone else you'd hit. I wouldn't care if you fell dead right now: at least I'd be sure you'd never look at anything beautiful again!'

The strange boy looked astonished. 'Why don't you fight, then?' he asked crossly.

'Because if I hit you back, I'd be no better than you are. I'd be just as rotten and worthless, and I'd have no right to be free!' The strange boy grinned at him, but there was a look of uncertainty about him and his eyes shifted uneasily. 'You're not all there!' he said. 'Who do you think you're talking to?'

'I don't think. I know. I'm talking to someone who likes brute force. And that's why I don't want to talk to you any more. You can hit me again if you can catch me!'

With that David jumped up smartly and ran off. He could not run very quickly because he was beginning to ache all over where the other had struck him. But the strange boy did not follow him: he only shouted, 'Idiot! You're a daft coward!' David had the impression that he was shouting so loudly for his own benefit.

ANNE HOLM

Once they wanted to play a game where some of them had to be soldiers and take the others prisoner.

'And I'll be captain over the soldiers!' shouted Carlo, hastily adding, 'That's if you don't want to be, David.'

David looked straight at him. 'I will not play anything evil and horrible,' he replied.

Maria said at once that if David would not play, she would not either, but Andrea said with some irritation, 'You're a strange chap, David. What's wicked about that?'

David waited until he was sure his voice would not tremble. 'I'm not very good at playing, but I can see when you play you try to imitate what's real, and I won't have anything to do with pretending to take people prisoner . . . it's horrible and evil. No one has any right to take other people prisoner. Everybody has a right to his life and freedom.'

'Yes, but, David' – Andrea's voice was no longer irritated, only interested – 'what if there's a murderer; shouldn't he be put in prison either? Or a thief, or something like that?'

David frowned. 'I don't know. Yes, a murderer, he should go to prison to stop him murdering more people; but no one should lay hands on him or starve him. No one has any right over other people.'

'Yes, but Father and Mother have a right over us,' Andrea said.

'No, it's not a right – at least, I don't think so. It's more of a . . . duty. I mean, since they're your parents, they must give you food and clothes, and teach you all the things you don't know, so that you can manage for yourselves when you're grown up. What they do is something good. That's not what I mean by right over people. Having right over others is something shameful. It's using force.'

ANNE HOLM

Every day brings us new chances
To enjoy the hours ahead,
Talking, learning, asking questions,
Till it's time to go to bed.

May our play be satisfying
And the hours with friends feel good.
Then, at night, when we are tired
We will know you've understood.

Hear us in the heat of quarrels,
When we want to think we're right;
Help us till we know our problems
Can be solved in calmer light.

Touch us in the quiet moments
When we need to know you're near;
Turn our longing into loving,
Take our trust, we know you're here.

LOIS M. AINGER

BIBLE READINGS

Psalm 46.8–11	—	He stamps out war
Isaiah 2.2–4	—	Spears into pruning hooks
Matthew 5.5, 7–10	—	True blessing
Matthew 5.21–24	—	Anger
Matthew 5.38–42	—	Turn the other cheek
James 4.1–2	—	Why we quarrel

Friends wanted

SEE ALSO:
49b,61b,62a,
80a,172b,173a,b,
174,175b

Alone

(*b*) No shelter, no clothes,
Always alone,
No parents, no love
And nowhere called home.

If only there was someone,
Someone to care,
Someone to give shelter
And something to wear.

Maybe one day their dream
May come true,
If someone helped out,
Someone like you.

DAWN GORDON (12 YEARS)

A boy

(*a*) Dingy carpets,
Rotted curtains,
Paper hanging
from the walls,
Water dripping
from the ceiling,
Forming wet and
dirty pools.

Long hair matted,
Shirt in tatters,
Trousers ripped and
patched at the knee,
Pockets missing,
Both socks ripping,
His face a picture of
endurance and grief.

Mother working,
Father shirking,
Four more children
still at school.
Another brother
Inside for murder.
Little chance of
proper food.

He's despised,
He's rejected,
In a broken and
disrupted home.
Makes one wonder
How he'll turn out,
In six or seven long
years' time.

MARK DODSWORTH
(15 YEARS)

When Jesus came to London,
He visited Hyde Park.
He gathered crowds around Him
And talked till it was dark
Of how we should remember
The homeless and the poor,
The hungry and exploited, that
We usually ignore.

They listened quietly to Him –
The strangest man they'd met –
Then each lit up his cigarette
And went home to forget!
They thought he was a preacher
Who'd tell them something nice!
Instead He ordered everyone
To practise sacrifice.

When Jesus came to London
They all knew what He meant,
But shrugged it off because the truth
Was inconvenient.
They packed Him off to Brixton
Where He could preach no more,
Then carried on in London town
Just like they did before.

PETER TONGEMAN

BIBLE READINGS

Deuteronomy 10.18–22	—	Care for strangers
Matthew 26.36–46	—	Jesus in need of friends
Luke 10.29–37	—	The Good Samaritan
Luke 19.1–10	—	Zacchæus
Acts 6.1–6	—	Care for widows

School and play

SEE ALSO:
32a,40a,b,
41b,42b,62a,
65,108a,142a,c

School in the early 20th Century

Our village school was poor and crowded, but in the end I relished it. It had a lively reek of steaming life: boys' boots, girls' hair, stoves and sweat, blue ink, white chalk, and shavings. We learnt nothing abstract or tenuous there – just simple patterns of facts and letters, portable tricks of calculation, no more than was needed to measure a shed, write out a bill, read a swine-disease warning. Through the dead hours of the morning, through the long afternoons, we chanted away at our tables. Passers-by could hear our rising voices in our bottled-up room on the bank; 'Twelve-inches – one-foot. Three-feet-make-a-yard. Fourteen-pounds-make-a stone. Eight-stone-a-hundred-weight.' We absorbed these figures as primal truths declared by some ultimate power. Unhearing, unquestioning, we rocked to our chanting, hammering the gold nails home. 'Twice-two-are-four. One-God-is-Love. One-Lord-is-King. One-King-is-George. One-George-is-Fifth . . .' So it was always; had been, would be for ever; we asked no questions; we didn't hear what we said; yet neither did we ever forget it.

LAURIE LEE

School in the days of Jesus

(*a*) Between the age of five and six the child began school, which was held often in the synagogue though there might be a special school house. Teacher and pupils either stood or sat in a semi-circle on the floor. The curriculum was divided into three phases: up to ten the boys learnt exclusively from the Old Testament; between ten and fifteen they were taught the traditional law; after fifteen they went on to study and discuss theology . . . there were no mathematics, nor physical education, nor music – elements considered essential by the Greeks.

PHYLLIS DOYLE

(*b*) What is this life if, full of care,
We have no time to stand and stare?

No time to stand beneath the boughs
And stare as long as sheep or cows.

No time to see, when woods we pass,
Where squirrels hide their nuts in grass.

No time to see, in broad daylight,
Streams full of stars like skies at night.

No time to turn at Beauty's glance,
And watch her feet, how they can dance.

No time to wait till her mouth can
Enrich that smile her eyes began.

A poor life this, if full of care,
We have no time to stand and stare.

W. H. DAVIES

Homework

(*a*) School is a drag when it follows you home
follows you into your room and waits for you
to come out of the toilet and sits waiting for
you to get through with your dinner
school work should not be done at home
homework sho'aint done at school I wonder what adult
made up this stupid 'homework' which is actually
schoolwork rule.

TED JOANS

(*b*) O Lord, Thou knowest how busy
I must be this day. If I forget
Thee, do not forget me.

JACOB ASTLEY 1579–1652

Only Eleven to Go

(*c*) Winsome, wistful, scathing of boys
And a little bit troubled when I play with toys
Yet happy with them.

From tiny primary to gigantic grammar.
New maths, new science, new French stammer.
Yet happy with them.

Sixth formers cruise like anonymous ships,
With boiler rooms full of exam tips.
And happy with them.

Now no brooding, moaning or salty tears,
I've only got another eleven years!
And happy with them?

FIONA TOMLINSON (AGED 11)

Monday morning

(*a*)
Father, five days of the week before us! There are bound to be experiences of sadness and joy in this week, times when work is hard and times when all seems easy, occasions when we enjoy the company of others and times when we would prefer to be alone. We pray that each hour of each day may help us to grow up, to understand life and ourselves better and live as useful members of the school. *Amen.*

First day of a new term

(*b*)
Eternal God, on this first day of a new term we give thanks for the holiday just ended and pray that the coming weeks may be useful and interesting in the life of the school.

Help us to welcome newcomers
  and to understand their uncertainty;
Help us to co-operate with each other
  and to work as one team in partnership;
Help us to work faithfully
  and make our separate contributions to the school-life.

As the weeks and terms go by, may we grow in understanding and knowledge. *Amen.*

End of a day or term

(*c*)
Father, at the end of this day/term we think of the life of our school and the part we each have played.
We offer you our successes and are glad of them.
We offer you the routine life of the school that makes up so much of the time we spend together.
We dare to offer you our failures believing that we have learned something because of them.
We gladly offer ourselves knowing your promise to use us in your work of love and care for the world. *Amen.*

(*a*) Two thousand lungs in unison,
A thousand mouths all yell as one,
Two weeks in Spain with glorious sun.
School's out until September.

A seething mass of boys and girls
Rush out as bedlam soon unfurls,
From peasant's son to little earl.
School's out until September.

The kids are full of expectation,
Rising glee and jubilation,
Full seven weeks for recreation.
School's out until September.

The teachers' gladness knows no bounds
They stand on strangely empty grounds,
For six more weeks no teenage sounds.
School's out until September.

IAN JOLLY (AGED 13)
Hewett School, Norwich

School's Out

(*b*) Girls scream,
Boys shout;
Dogs bark,
School's out.

Cats run,
Horses shy;
Into trees
Birds fly.

Babes wake
Open-eyed;
If they can,
Tramps hide.

Old man,
Hobble home;
Merry mites,
Welcome.

W. H. DAVIES

Holidays

(*a*) Holidays, as we know them, are a modern invention. Even last century very few ordinary people went away for a week or fortnight's holiday. Travel was difficult and expensive and there were many people who never left the village in which they had been born. Few working people had more than the occasional day off work – and worked nine or ten hours a day as well in some cases.

Most of the occasional days off work were for religious festivals like Christmas and Easter and these broke the year for the workers who otherwise would have had no rest day at all except Sunday.

No work was done on these religious festivals because, to celebrate the life of Jesus, they were called holy days. Holy days became holidays and have developed into the much longer breaks from work that we know today.

(*b*) We thank You, Father, for the excitement of a holiday,
For the eager looking forward,
For the great day itself when off we go.
For the adventure of exploring a new place,
or the joy of renewing acquaintance with the old.
For the fun and the games,
For friendships new and old,
For parents and loved ones who make it possible,
and who share in our happiness,
We thank You, our Father. *Amen.*

J. & E. YOUNG

BIBLE READINGS

Exodus 12.21–27	}	Teaching the generation
Deuteronomy 6.4–9	}	
Exodus 35.1–2	—	The gift of the holy day
Zechariah 8.3–5	—	Playtime in a city of peace
Matthew 11.16–17	—	Children's play helps Jesus to teach

TOWN AND AROUND

THEME COMMENT

We have readily produced a theology of the countryside. Both Old and New Testaments created the necessary momentum for they were written in ages when the majority of the people lived in rural communities.

We have not yet come to terms with the industrial revolution nor outgrown the ancient obsession which views the city as a wicked place. Sodom and Gomorrah still colour our thinking. But the vision of the city as a place of glory and hope is not absent from the Bible. Jerusalem is exalted, of course, since it holds the temple but Abraham looks for a city with foundations, Ezekiel draws up plans of an acceptable temple for a new city and the Book of Revelation hopes for better things in a new Jerusalem.

The twentieth century lives in cities. When they subject people to a style of life which is crippling, then they stand under Christian judgment, but our criticism should not be too hasty. So long as there are homeless we cannot sneer at high-rising flats, and a consumer society cannot dismiss factories. Remembering modern transport needs, there is much to make us rejoice in the stretch of tarmac that has replaced the cart-track.

One of our Christian tasks is to help children to discern the beauty in the city and encourage builders to promote it. There is an elegance in many modern buildings which we too readily condemn and a perfection of line in motorway and its bridges to which we must not be blind.

Our greater task, rejecting a false nostalgia which looks back to 'ideal' village communities, is to explore the meaning of community in the city. Community centres, the local church, the Health and Social Services, voluntary schemes and simple neighbourliness will all be features of this. The fact is that, like it or not, we are city-dwellers and our theology of creation, which can no longer be derived from the village duckpond, must find its sources in the city.

(*a*) Do you feel more comfortable among lamp-posts than among ash-poles? The late Lady Cunard hated the country: 'All those trees and fields make me feel *dizzy*'. . . .

After all, most of our population live in towns. Isn't a landscape of roof-tops, petrol pumps and neon signs more 'natural' to most people than downs and wooded valleys and thatched cottages? More natural in the sense that that's their territory, the surroundings they've grown up among, know best and feel most at home in?

KENNETH ALLSOP

Towns and cities

(*b*) All things bright and beautiful
All creatures great and small;
All things wise and wonderful,
The Lord God made them all.

The fountains' water spouting,
The trees in city square;
The flowers in window boxes
And shrubs by hotel doors.

The ducks and swans and pigeons,
The poodles and the cats;
The great beasts in their cages,
And guinea pigs in flats.

The leaves that fall in autumn
In shades of red and brown;
The wind that blows them on the paths
Of parks about our town.

The clouds above the rooftops,
The ever-changing light;
The sun that dries the pavements
When rain sweeps down at night.

YVONNE TOMES

SEE ALSO:
30b,32b,91a,
93,94,95a,
96a,145a

(*a*) Are buildings sacred? Of course not. Buildings on average have a life not much longer than that of human beings.

By the end of much the same time span most are decrepit, out-of-date and unfit for modern use. Unless they can readily be improved or converted or have a marked historical or architectural interest, they should be demolished and replaced.

Britain has a huge stock of over-age senile buildings. . . . Of our 14 million occupied houses, 2½ million are more than 100 years old. Thousands of acres are an abandoned wilderness of derelict mills, works and slag heaps – areas which have finished their working life. By 1980 a total of nearly 4 million houses built before 1880 will be obsolete. 500,000 of them are declared slums; another 2 million lack fixed bath and about as many don't have exclusive use of a lavatory.

KENNETH ALLSOP

(*b*) Skipping down the pavement wide,
Count the paving stones;
Big or small, or square or round,
See their patterns on the ground!
House and factory; church and shop,
Bricks and stones built high:
Busy workmen make them all:
See the patterns on each wall!

People walking down the street,
Dressed in colours gay;
Stripes and circles, frills and bows:
See the patterns in their clothes!
Clouds and sunshine, night-time stars,
Clothes and curtains too;
Stones and pavement, bricks and wall:
See the patterns in them all!

(*a*) The lights go up all over the town,
And the sun is going slowly down,
Making the pavements red as roses,
Making the children sleepy;

Golden the window lights are glowing,
Bright through the dusk the traffic's flowing.
God bless the people homeward going,
God be with us in Our Town.

The blinds come down in all of the shops,
The sparrows fly from the chimney tops;
High overhead go flocks of starlings
Home to their roosting places;

Through all the alleys dusk is creeping,
Over the rooftops stars come peeping.
God bless the children gently sleeping,
God be with us in Our Town.

M. E. ROSE

(*b*) I like the town on rainy nights
When everything is wet –
When all the town has magic lights
And streets of shining jet.

When all the rain about the town
Is like a looking glass,
And all the lights are upside down
Below me as I pass.

In all the pools are velvet skies,
And down the dazzling street
A fairy city gleams and lies
In beauty at my feet.

IRENE THOMPSON

(*a*) Pressing each upon the other
in the city
are wealth and poverty,
glamour and squalor,
gay lights and dark alleys,
hygienic wonders of glass, steel and concrete
and crumbling, rat-infested slums.

There is haste in the city,
in the office, in the street.
Shoulders jostle in the city,
but people rarely meet;
people throng the city,
but in the midst is loneliness.

EDMUND BANYARD

(*b*) The fullness of the earth is God's alone
and life's unfolding is divinely known.
With humble hearts we recognise the claim
that every child and nation bears his name.

Not only his a world of field and flower;
to him belongs the scene of stack and tower.
His love is focused on the city street,
and on canteens where busy people meet.

On wards and sites, in workshops and in schools,
in work of mind and skilfulness with tools,
we feel his presence in our daily round:
the place on which we stand is holy ground.

Then let us every given morning pray
that we may sanctify the city's day;
that Christ may guard our going out and in
and choose through us the world in love to win.

FRED KAAN

Now is the time to live,
to come to the Father who creates us,
to sing to the Lord who frees us,
to dance with the Spirit who fills us.

Let us invite the city
to worship with us.

We call the traffic in the streets,
department stores,
revolving doors,
and all the people
in the yellow pages,
to stop and shout his name.

Let us invite our leaders
to glorify his name.

We summon doctor, politician, star,
president, professor, clown,
to step down
and kneel with us.

Let us invite the injured people
to speak with us.

We ask all people, living alone,
the blacks and the whites
who have no rights,
the unemployed and angry poor,
to tell the truth in love.

Let us extend an open invitation
to one and all
to join in one full circle of joy.

Join the circle, Lord,
and make our joy complete.

NORMAN C. HABEL (adapted)

I want to remember with You, God,
Some lovely things people have enjoyed today,
And say Thank You, for us all.

Brightness of sunshine, perhaps,
Or wind tugging our hair,
The way the TV aerials stand tall and high over the houses,
The way the petals of a flower are arranged round the gold centre,
The different greenness of grass and of tree,
The bright colours in shop windows,
And the neat rows of packets and tins in the supermarket;
The red and amber and gold of the traffic lights,
The taste of good meals,
Or the smell of the garden after rain.
These and a thousand other lovely things
I remember now, with You.
I'll tell You some of the special ones I've noticed . . .

Thank you for lovely things, God.
Keep me on the look out for them,
Give everybody joy in them. *Amen.*

LILIAN COX

BIBLE READINGS

Genesis 18.16–33	—	Pleading for a city
Psalm 107.35–38	}	Deserts reclaimed
Isaiah 35.1–10	}	Deserts reclaimed
Psalm 127	—	Except the Lord build . . .
Luke 19.41–44	—	Tears for a city
Hebrews 11.8–10	—	A city with foundations
Revelation 21.1–4	—	Vision of a city

Countryside

SEE ALSO:
10b, 28a, 38, 49a, 70b, 101, 102a, 104b, 106a, b, 108b, 109a, b, 146a, b, 150b

I live in a town, and the country calls
In voices sweet and green –
Bird song and rippling stream
And leaves, fresh and clean.

The tumbling splash of the waterfalls,
A blue kingfisher's dart
As it turns on the wing;
And the hedger's art.

A thatched straw roof; thick ivy on old walls;
Dark woods; an ancient church
Guarding forgotten graves.
Tender buds of birch.

Rough, towering elms; purple loosestrife tall;
Softly caressing boughs.
A fox, a snake, birds' nests
And gentle grazing cows.

I live in a town, and the country calls
To all that I have seen
Of God's good earth, unspoiled,
Beautiful and clean.

PETER TONGEMAN

I sing the hills of the South land,
  From Wessex to Weald of Kent:
The springy turf of the downland,
  With bracing, pungent scent.
Thank God for the gift of the chalk land,
  White cliff and gorse and Ring;
For ancient barrow and beacon –
  The hills of the South I sing.

I sing the hills of the North land,
  Northumbria's fortress wall:
The grey, steep crags of the Border,
  And heather's purple pall.
Thank God for the hills of the North land,
  Great Cheviot, Simonside;
For wind-swept summit and moorland,
  The Ottercops wild and wide.

I sing the hills of the West land,
  From Malvern to Devon shores:
Of Cotswolds fair and the Mendips;
  And Dartmoor's rocky tors.
Then East I will sing of the Clevelands,
  Of Yorkshire moors and Wolds;
For all show forth in their beauty
  The treasure our island holds.

Thank God who gave us this England,
  With hills for her crown and pride:
The Pennines, Peak to High Cross Fell,
  With Pendle and Great Whernside:
And, noblest, the summits of Lakeland,
  Helvellyn, Scafell tall –
I lift my eyes to the hilltops
  In praise to the Lord of all.

ALBERT F. BAYLY

(*a*) Heather's out on the hillside;
Purple cloak cast round
The shoulders broad and arms outflung
Of moors green gowned.
Heather borders the farm-track
Climbing over the ridge
To a lonely house by wind-swept trees,
And the burn beneath a bridge.

Hives are up on the heather:
Honey calls the bees.
The tall grass sings and bracken bows
Before the breeze.
Fleeting shadows of cloud-ships
Race from valley to hill:
And the winds from God's wide spaces give
Of their life my soul to fill.

ALBERT F. BAYLY

(*b*) Lord, open our eyes to see your work around us:
in the towering spectacle of great mountains
and the intricate beauty of the wayside flower;
in the fast-roaring torrent of the waterfall,
and the lazy gliding stream;
in the broad plains stretching mile upon mile,
and the woodland glade, the sheltered cove;
in the lush fields of agriculture,
and the sparse, dry moorland.
Lord, open our eyes to see your work around us. *Amen.*

BIBLE READINGS

Leviticus 26.3–7 — A land of plenty
Psalm 65.9–13 — Pastures and hills
Matthew 6.25–34 } Nature speaks of God
Romans 1.19–20 }

People

SEE ALSO:
12,16,17,25a,
26,41a,44a,47a,48

(*a*) He made the people that I meet,
The many people, great and small,
In home and school, and down the street,
And he made me to love them all.

J. M. C. CRUM

(*b*) As I run down the street in the winter,
As I walk through the park in the spring,
All the people I meet have a secret,
For each one is the son of a King.

From the milkman collecting his bottles,
To the boy swinging high on his swing,
They belong to our heavenly Father;
So each one is the son of a King.

And wherever the people may come from
– Say, Jamaica, Dundee or Peking –
We can look for a family likeness,
For they all are the sons of a King.

So whenever we greet other people,
As we go through the world wandering,
We must give them our trust and affection,
For each one is the son of our King.

M. E. ROSE

There are all kinds of men
Who have done me good turns,
That I still never think about,
Not for a minute;
Yet if I were making up
That sort of grace,
They would all of them have
To be in it.

One man made up stories,
Another wrote verses
I found, and I liked,
And I read till I knew them.
Another one saw
All the things they had written,
Then, being an artist,
He drew them.

Another took wood
And a saw and some glue,
And put each of them just
In the place that would need it;
So that is the chair
Where I sit with my book
And am so much at ease
As I read it.

I'm forgetting the one
Who read tale after tale
When I was too young
To know letter from letter,
And the other who taught me them,
Till in the end
I could read for myself –
Which was better.

RODNEY BENNETT

(*a*) A person can never get true greatness by paying for it. It is nice to have good clothes, it makes it a lot easier to act decent, but it is a sign of true greatness to act decent when you have not got them, just as good as if you had.

One time, when mother was a little girl, they had a bird at their house called Bill that broke its leg. They thought they would have to kill him, but next morning they found him, sort of sideways on his good leg – singing. That was true greatness.

Once there was a woman that had done a big washing and hung it on the line. The line broke and let it all down in the mud, but she did not say a word, only did it all over again. This time she spread it on the grass where it could not fall; but that night a dog with dirty feet ran over it. All she said was, "Aint it queer that he did not miss nothing". That was true greatness. But it is only people that have done washing that know it.

ANON. Written by a schoolgirl aged 13, in 1913

(*b*) Father, we know that all the world belongs to You and all the people in it are Your great family. You do not ask where people live, whether they have brown, black or white skins, whether they live in big houses or small, are strong or weak, clever or ordinary. You love all of them, all over the world, all the time. We rejoice that all people have a God and Father like You and a Friend like Jesus. *Amen.*

(*a*) Here is a man who was born in an obscure village, the child of a peasant woman. He worked in a carpenter's shop until he was thirty, and then for three years he was an itinerant preacher. He had no credentials but himself. While still a young man, the tide of popular opinion turned against him. His friends – the twelve men who had learned so much from him, and had promised him their enduring loyalty – ran away, and left him. He went through a mockery of a trial; he was nailed upon a cross between two thieves; when he was dead, he was taken down and laid in a borrowed grave through the pity of a friend.

Yet I am well within the mark when I say that all the armies that ever marched, and all the parliaments that ever sat, and all the kings that ever reigned, put together, have not affected the life of man upon this earth as has this one solitary life.

ANON

(*b*) In eighteen hundred eighty eight
Michael Robbins made a gate;
Struck it true and struck it straight.

Michael Robbins, hale and free,
As fine a man as you might see;
Smith and sexton both was he.

"Praise God from whom all blessings flow!"
He sang. The gate began to grow.
"Praise Him, all creatures here below!"

Simple, gentle, sturdy, kind
Michael Robbins left behind
Treasure for the honest mind;
For while the wind goes shouting by,
And men are born, grow old and die,
His gate stands talking to the sky.

M. J. MARTYN

Seeing Jesus in people

God abides in men
because Christ has put on
the nature of man, like a garment,
and worn it to His own shape.
He has put on everyone's life.
He has fitted Himself to the little child's dress,
to the shepherd's coat of sheepskin,
to the workman's coat,
to the king's red robes,
to the snowy loveliness of the wedding garment,
and to the drab
of the sad simple battle-dress.
He has given man His crown,
the thorn that is jewelled
with drops of His blood.
He has fastened His hands
to the tree of life.
He has latched his feet
in crimson sandals,
that they move not
from the path of love.
God abides in man.

CARYLL HOUSELANDER

BIBLE READINGS

Genesis 1.26–28	—	In the image of God
Matthew 10.2–4	—	The twelve disciples
Luke 6.28–31 James 2.1–4	}	How to treat people
John 1.6–14	—	A light to enlighten every man
Romans 16.1–15	—	A list of Christ's servants
1 Corinthians 12.14–26	—	Everybody needs everybody

People and their work

SEE ALSO:
14a,15b,32b, 71a,b,72a,109a, 142b,143c,159b

(*a*) Like a great river flow the people
Into the town at break of day:
Men building homes
Or making toys;
Cleaners and cooks
And office boys;
Watch them at evening, work all over,
Eagerly take their homeward way.

M. E. ROSE

Going to work in 1823

(*b*) David Livingstone started (work) at the age of ten. Previous biographers have glossed over the conditions in which he worked and represented them as a suitably rigorous upbringing for a future explorer. The reality was very different. All employers at Blantyre Mills, both adults and children, worked from six in the morning till eight at night, with half an hour for breakfast and an hour for lunch: a working day of twelve and a half hours, six days a week. . . .

Three-quarters of the work force at Blantyre were children, and most of these, like Livingstone, were employed as 'piecers', their job being to piece together threads on the spinning frames if they looked like breaking. . . . Piecers needed sharp eyes and the power of constant attention if they were to avoid frequent beatings. They also had to be unusually agile since their work often involved climbing under the machinery or balancing over it. Piecers walked anything up to twenty miles a day in the mills and much of this distance was covered crawling or stooping.

TIM JEAL

Shopkeepers

(*a*) I know all the shops along the street –
The draper sells clothes, the butcher sells meat.
The toyshop sells all our favourite toys,
Dollies for girls and train sets for boys.
We see in the hardware stores brushes and mops,
Baking tins, floor polish, clothes pegs and props.
The stationer has pens, paper and ink to show,
And all kinds of cards, set out in a row.
The greengrocer sells fruit and vegetables green,
The jeweller, necklaces fit for a queen.
The grocer sells food, for you and for me –
Bacon for breakfast and jam for our tea.
The chemist sells medicine, tablets and pills,
The milliner, hats, with feathers and frills.
Haberdashery has ribbons, buttons and bows,
Needles and cotton – as everyone knows.

E. W. STANTON

(*b*) The bricklayer laid a brick on the bed of cement,
Then, with a precise stroke of his trowel, spread another layer
And, without a by-your-leave, laid on another brick.
The foundations grew visibly,
The building rose, tall and strong, to shelter men.

I thought, Lord, of that brick buried in the darkness at the base of the big building.
No one sees it, but it accomplishes its task, and the other bricks need it.
Lord, what difference whether I am on the roof-top or in the foundations of your building, as long as I stand faithfully at the right place?

MICHEL QUOIST

Different people; different jobs

Most of the people at the school I went to had an ambition to be bank clerks, doctors and things like that. But *printing* always fascinated me right from the beginning, and I made up my mind to go into it six months before I finished at school. It's very interesting – you're doing different things all the time, and one day a week I go down to the London College of Printing to learn more about the theoretical side of it.

> Arrived at the firm at 7.55. Sat down
> at my bench and started repairing a pair
> of Georgian candlesticks which were made
> in the year 1759 by James Gould. First I
> took the bottom off and then ran the rosin
> out of them. Then I burnt them out and
> pickled them – pickle consisting of eight
> parts water and one part sulphuric acid.
> I left them in the pickle for about fifteen
> minutes and then rinsed them under water
> and dried them out. Then with a colet
> hammer I tapped the bruises out of them
> and burnished them. Then, using easyflow
> flux and easyflow solder, I filled in the
> holes and pickled them again to remove the
> flux. . . . I got the candlesticks out of
> the pickle again and filed them up, filled
> them with rosin and sent them down for
> sanding and polishing ready for plating. . . .
> At 4.50 p.m. I had a wash and left work
> at five o'clock. (*A silversmith*)

I like the *butchery trade* very much. It gets you full of grease and it makes you smell a bit when you come home, but it's a good life – open air, you're in the shop and you meet people. It's really interesting, never monotonous. The most important thing about a job is getting to the top – mastering the whole lot.

ALL ABOVE ITEMS BY PETER WILLMOTT

BRAZIL	Growing coffee, oranges, nuts, sugar, tobacco, cocoa, rubber and cotton employs many people. There are also cattle ranches in the south. Brazil has many minerals, so factories are also being built.
CARIBBEAN	Some of the towns-people work in factories; many help in mining bauxite which is made into aluminium. Oil is found in Trinidad. Village people work on the land growing coconuts, sugar, bananas, coffee and cotton.
KENYA	Many people work on the land growing coffee, tea and sisal for rope-making. Factories are needed for these products. Hides and skins are exported. Salt is collected from Lake Magadi.
NORTH INDIA	Living in villages the majority work on the land, but many have no jobs. Factories are being built in cities.
SOUTH INDIA	Many people work in textile mills, mines, paddy fields and on tea plantations. Mines yield magnesium, iron, bauxite and gold. Factories spin cotton.
HONG KONG	'Made in Hong Kong' is a well-known mark on many clothes, toys and electrical goods sold in this country. One of the most crowded places in the world, it has very many light industries to employ people.
ZAMBIA	The second largest source of copper in the world, Zambia employs many miners. Farm workers produce maize, and groundnuts. The large lakes give employment to fishermen.

(Information taken from *Getting to Know* leaflets)

God in man's work

(*a*) In quest for knowledge, truth and skill
We trace a great creator's will;
In mill and market, school and street,
The ground is holy where we meet.

In workshop sounds, in engines strong,
We hear an echo of his song:
On dock and building site, in mine,
True work fulfils a scheme divine.

New ways of healing now he shows;
Through caring hands God's blessing flows;
His science aids the farmer's toil
As food springs forth from fertile soil.

Atom and Universe proclaim
The source of life our lips can name;
We who his greater glory share
Will by our lives his love declare.

ALAN OGLE

The missionary

(*b*) "This is for life. Through thick and thin. Whether it's comfortable or whether it isn't. Whether I'm thanked or not. Whether it's dangerous or not."

This is what 'missionary' means to Stephen Carr. Because of this he will try his hand at anything. He will dirty his knees. He will drive himself with a remorselessness that few other men would comprehend. He recently turned down a job at £14,000 a year, tax free. When bad luck plunged his only tractor 300 feet to destruction and anyone else would have sat back and waited for a replacement, he and his workers head-loaded the 50 tons of vitally needed young seedlings over 12 miles of bush.

HELEN & RICHARD EXLEY

Night workers

(*a*) Lights go up at night in the city
People sleep while life is still busy.

Newspapers roll off the printing machines,
The over-night jet from the runway screams,
Doctors and nurses do late duty call,
An ambulance races to hospital.

Bakers prepare for tomorrow's bread,
A nightwatchman sits in his tiny shed,
Shift-workers pause for a first cup of tea,
The trawlerman hauls his catch from the sea.

ANTHONY GEERING

A fisherman's prayer

(*b*) Protect me, O Lord;
My boat is so small,
And your sea so big.

BIBLE READINGS

1 Kings 7.13–22	—	Designer in metal
Job 28.1–4, 9–11	—	Miners
Psalm 107.23–32	—	Those who go down to the sea
Proverbs 6.6–11	—	The ant as an example
Jeremiah 18.1–5	—	The potter
Matthew 4.18–22; 9.9	}	The disciples' jobs
Acts 18.1–4		

ALL THE YEAR ROUND

THEME COMMENT

The Lord said within himself:

> While the earth lasts
> seedtime and harvest, cold and heat,
> summer and winter, day and night,
> shall never cease.

Genesis 8.22

The process of thought which led to these words is interesting. The process is scientific; the conclusion theological. The author had observed the seasons and had deduced a regular pattern in the changing year. He arrives at a 'natural law' that spring, summer, autumn and winter proceed in regular procession and day can be relied on to follow night. In the complex and changing circumstances of his life these are discerned as 'dependables'. It is a scientific observation and conclusion requiring the same skill as that of contemporary scientists who observe, collate experiences and then deduce 'laws' or patterns.

The author then takes a leap of faith which turns him from a scientist into a theologian. He reads into his experience the conviction that an eternal and personal promise lies behind the observed pattern. He cannot prove it as he might prove that roses bloom in June, but it becomes an article of faith to live by.

When we help our children to discern the patterns of day and night and the seasons, they are engaged in a process which is at one and the same time scientific and theological. We will not encourage the crude response 'because the seasons are dependable, God is dependable', otherwise faith falls with the first experience of a summer frost or high temperatures in December. But the dependability of the natural world (as the dependability of human friendship) will offer significant clues in our shared discovery of a God who will never forsake his people.

Day and night

SEE ALSO:
29b,72a,c,
79a,b,105a

(*a*) Said Day to Night,
'I bring God's light.
What gift have you?'
Night said, 'The dew.'

'I give bright hours,'
Quoth Day, 'and flowers.'
Said Night, 'More blest,
I bring sweet rest.'

ANN LINDSAY

When I Wake Up

(*b*) Good-morning, God!
You're giving me today:
Your things to do,
Your words to say.
Today's a new path
I haven't yet trod:
But You'll be with me –
Good-morning, God!

Before I Go To Sleep

(*c*) Dear God, good-night;
I'm bringing You my day,
Some things golden,
Some things grey,
I'm still with You;
We'll turn out the light.
Forgive me, love me;
Dear God, good-night.

SOURCE UNKNOWN

(*d*) On the wings of the morning,
On the gleam of the day,
On the silver dawning
Of the sun's first ray
The light rides in – so night depart
And the Lord of Light possess my heart.

BREMER HOFMEYR

(*a*) Getting up is generally a bit of a rush, even if you wake early. A lot of people would say, 'There just isn't time to say prayers'. But God never stops thinking of US, and we can think of him whatever we are doing, whether getting out of bed, washing, dressing, going down to breakfast, or seeing that pets are fed.

There is an old story about two men who were talking about praying. They were sure that to pray you must be in a certain position, either kneeling or standing, and that you could not pray in any other way. They were interrupted by another man who told them of an accident he had one day when he fell down a well. 'And,' he said, 'the prayingest prayer I ever prayed was standing on my head.' So we can think of God, and thank him and love him, at any time.

From *Time and Again* prayers

(*b*) The earth not only moves round the sun, taking one year for each orbit, it also spins on its own axis. As the sun is in a fixed position this means that each part of the earth is facing the sun at one time each 24 hours and is turned away from the sun at another time. Facing the sun we receive its light; that is our day. Turned away from the sun we cannot receive its light; that is our night.

BIBLE READINGS

Genesis 1.14–18	—	Separate day from night
Psalm 74.16–17	—	God's gift of day and night
Psalm 104.19–23	—	Creatures of day and night
Psalm 121	—	He never slumbers, never sleeps
Psalm 139.11–12	—	God is in day and night

Twelve months

January brings the snow,
Makes our feet and fingers glow.

February brings the rain,
Thaws the frozen lake again.

March brings breezes, loud and shrill,
To stir the dancing daffodil.

April brings the primrose sweet,
Scatters daisies at our feet.

May brings flocks of pretty lambs,
Skipping by their fleecy dams.

June brings tulips, lilies, roses,
Fills the children's hands with posies.

Hot July brings cooling showers,
Apricots and gillyflowers.

August brings the sheaves of corn,
Then the harvest home is borne.

Warm September brings the fruit;
Sportsmen then begin to shoot.

Fresh October brings the pheasant;
Then to gather nuts is pleasant.

Dull November brings the blast;
Then the leaves are whirling fast.

Chill December brings the sleet,
Blazing fire, and Christmas treat.

SARA COLERIDGE

SEE ALSO:
104b,*105b*,
113

Weathers

(*a*) This is the weather the cuckoo likes,
And so do I;
When showers betumble the chestnut spikes,
And nestlings fly:
And the little brown nightingale bills his best,
And they sit outside at "The Traveller's Rest",
And maids come forth sprig-muslin drest,
And citizens dream of the south and west,
And so do I.

This is the weather the shepherd shuns,
And so do I;
When beeches drip in browns and duns,
And thresh, and ply;
And hill-hid tides throb, throe on throe,
And meadow rivulets overflow,
And drops on gate-bars hang in a row,
And rooks in families homeward go,
And so do I.

THOMAS HARDY

(*b*) Lightning is an electric spark cracking through the air. Thunder is the noise the spark makes. They both happen at the same time but it takes the light hardly any time at all to travel to the ground. The noise of the thunder travels at 750 miles an hour. Therefore, an observer on the ground hears the thunder several seconds after seeing the lightning. 750 mph is about 5 seconds for each mile so, if you count the seconds between seeing the lightning and hearing the thunder and divide this number by five you will discover how far away the storm is.

(*a*) Do you feel sad when Christmas is done?
No more parties and no more fun.
No more parcels or Christmas holly
Or paper chains that look so jolly?

That's when I think of the next nice things:
Snowballs and Easter eggs, catkins and spring,
Pantomimes, circuses, trips to the zoo,
Birthdays with parties, and holidays too;

Building sandcastles and dips in the sea;
Then autumn and conkers, and crumpets for tea;
And all of a sudden, the winter's begun,
With the fifth of November and fireworks and fun.

The shops become full
Of bright gifts and good cheer;
And then – yes you've guessed it!
Next Christmas is here!

ELISABETH BARRETT

(*b*) The earth moves in two ways. First, it spins on its own axis thus making night and day. Secondly it circles round the sun in a planned orbit. There is nothing special about that. All the nine planets move in their own track or orbit and at their own speed. The nearer their orbit is to the sun the faster they travel. Mercury is the nearest and circles the sun in three months. Pluto is the most distant and takes about 250 years to complete one orbit. Earth is 93 million miles from the sun and takes one year to make its journey around the sun.

BIBLE READINGS

Genesis 8.22	—	The reliability of the seasons
Psalm 102.23–28	—	God's years have no end

The Seasons—

Spring

SEE ALSO:

33a,49a, 86b,126b,143b

(*a*) SPRING
came
with the
wind
to revive the
dormant flame . . .
LIFE
can
rise again.

ALICE A. GORGE

(*b*) *March*

The cock is crowing,
The stream is flowing,
The small birds twitter,
The lake doth glitter,
The green field sleeps in the sun;
The oldest and youngest
Are at work with the strongest;
The cattle are grazing,
Their heads never raising;
There are forty feeding like one!

Like an army defeated
The snow hath retreated,
And now doth fare ill
On the top of the bare hill;
The ploughboy is whooping -anon-anon:
There's joy in the mountains;
There's life in the fountains;
Small clouds are sailing,
Blue skies prevailing;
The rain is over and gone!

WILLIAM WORDSWORTH

(*a*) The year's at the spring,
And day's at the morn;
Morning's at seven;
The hillside's dew pearled;
The lark's on the wing;
The snail's on the thorn:
God's in his heaven –
All's right with the world!

ROBERT BROWNING

(*b*) Seeds, bursting from their winter sleep,
Run, their appointed hour to keep.
They strive and thrust, they twist and run,
To lift their hearts towards the sun.
Seeds in their silent winter bed
They lay as cold and still as dead,
Beneath the stiff, white sheets of frost,
Their bodies empty shells and lost.
Beneath the deep, soft quilt of snow
They waited, row on sleeping row;
And when the fingers of the thaw
Tapped gently at each hidden door,
They stirred, the seeds no man can number,
Yet turned again to dark and slumber
Till the first trumpets of the sun,
Tilted to heaven, afresh begun
Their song of spring. The seeds awoke,
Shook off their hard and heavy yoke
Of clay and stone, then, furrow-free,
Leapt to fulfil their destiny.

PETER HOWARD

Summer

(*a*) Summer is fun!
The birds are singing,
The flowers are swinging,
The day's begun.

Summer is fun!
The winter is over,
Spring brings the clover,
And summer the sun.

SARAH HOMBRAY (AGED 9)

(*b*) We sat by the roadside and scooped the dust with our hands and made little piles in the gutters. Then we slid through the grass and lay on our backs and just stared at the empty sky. There was nothing to do. Nothing moved or happened, nothing happened at all except summer. Small heated winds blew over our faces, dandelion seeds floated by, burnt sap and roast nettles tingled our nostrils together with the dull rust smell of dry ground. The grass was June high and had come up with a rush, a massed entanglement of species, crested with flowers and spears of wild wheat, and coiled with clambering vetches, the whole of it humming with blundering bees and flickering with scarlet butterflies. Chewing grass on our backs, the grass scaffolding the sky, the summer was all we heard; cuckoos crossed distances on chains of cries, flies buzzed and choked in the ears, and the saw-toothed chatter of mowing-machines drifted on waves of air from the fields.

LAURIE LEE

Cuckoo

(*a*) Sumer is icumen in,
Lhude sing cuccu;
Groweth sed and bloweth med
And springth the wude nu.
Sing cuccu!
Awe bleteth after lomb,
Lhouth after calve cu;
Balluc sterteth, bucke verteth;
Murie sing cuccu.
Cuccu, cuccu,
Wel singes thu, cuccu,
Ne swik thu naver nu.

ANON. Written about 1225

Lhouth – loweth
Verteth – rest in the green
Swik – cease

Out of doors

(*b*) For the heat of the sun,
For the cool of the rain,
For the blue water's run,
For the green of the lane,
We thank You, heavenly Father.

For the sand on the beach,
For the gulls on the cliff,
For the slow river's reach,
For the salt sea's whiff,
We thank You, heavenly Father.

J. & E. YOUNG

Summer holiday

(*a*) Some time to wander and reflect
On life. Some time to laze.
Some time to stroll gaily bedecked
In summer clothes through ways
Unhurried. Some time to ask at leisure –
"Where shall we go?" Or lie
And watch a spider's artful measure
Entrap a passing fly.

Some time to tread soft, springing grass
And walk where flowers enrich
The multi-scented earth. Or pass
By shimmering trees which
Shelter shrill birds in joyful song.
To brave the tumbling sea,
Or skip through chilling foam along
The shore and shout with glee.

Some time to hear, to feel, to see
Such natural beauty, sets men free;
Each sense elated by the spell
Of him whose touch made all things well.

PETER TONGEMAN

(*b*) For flowers that bloom about our feet,
For tender grass, so fresh, so sweet,
For song of bird, and hum of bee,
For all things fair we hear or see
We thank Thee, heavenly Father.

For blue of stream, and blue of sky,
For pleasant shade of branches high,
For fragrant air and cooling breeze,
For beauty of the blooming trees
We thank Thee, heavenly Father.

RALPH W. EMERSON

Autumn

(*a*) With many new machines now
We do the work each day:
We reap the fields with combines,
We bale the new mown hay.
But it is God who gives us
Inventive skills and drives
Which lighten labour's drudgery
And give us fuller lives.

Author unknown

(*b*) I was awake, I could see, I was happy. I lay looking out of the small green window. The world outside was crimson and on fire. I had never seen it looking like that before.

'Doth?' I said, 'what's happening to them trees?'

Dorothy was dressing. She leaned out of the window, slow and sleepy, and the light came through her nightdress like sand through a sieve.

'Nothing's happening,' she said.

'Yes it is then,' I said. 'They're falling to bits.'

Dorothy scratched her dark head, yawning wide, and white feathers floated out of her hair.

'It's only the leaves droppin'. We're in autumn now. The leaves always drop in autumn.'

Autumn? In autumn. Was that where we were? Where the leaves always dropped and there was always this smell. I imagined it continuing, with no change, for ever, these wet flames of woods burning on and on like the bush of Moses, as natural a part of this new found land as the eternal snows of the poles. Why had we come to such a place?

LAURIE LEE

(*a*) Now join we, to praise the creator,
our voices in worship and song;
we stand to recall with thanksgiving
that to him all seasons belong.

We thank you, O God, for your goodness,
for the joy and abundance of crops,
for food that is stored in our larders,
for all we can buy in the shops.

But also of need and starvation
we sing with concern and despair,
of skills that are used for destruction,
of land that is burnt and laid bare.

We cry for the plight of the hungry
while harvests are left on the field,
for orchards neglected and wasting,
for produce from markets withheld.

The song grows in depth and in wideness:
the earth and its people are one.
There can be no thanks without giving,
no words without deeds that are done.

Then teach us, O Lord of the harvest,
to be humble in all that we claim;
to share what we have with the nations,
to care for the world in your name.

FRED KAAN

(*b*) For the mellow colours of autumn,
For ripened fruits and harvest stored,
For the first touch of frost cleansing the earth,
For the anticipation of winter and its sports,
For the rhythm of the changing seasons
Thanks be to God who gives all that is good.

(*a*) Long, crusty loaves of twisted shapes,
A bowl of eggs, a bunch of grapes;
Michaelmas daisies, mauve and blue,
Gay marigolds and asters too;
A jar of honey, a jug of milk,
Peaches with skins like softest silk;
A box of apples, a bag of plums,
A bunch of bronze chrysanthemums;
Blackberries on a leafy dish,
Marrows as large as you could wish;
A pound of butter, a piece of ham,
A round red cheese, and strawberry jam;
A cabbage with fine, curling leaves,
Wheat, oats and barley in full sheaves;
Baskets of peas still wet with dew,
And runner beans all crisp and new;
Onions, potatoes, carrots, leeks,
Hips and haws with glowing cheeks;
Curved cucumbers, tomatoes red,
And celery with curly head;
Bunches of mint that smell so good,
And gold-fringed bracken from the wood:
For all these things we want to say
Thank you, God, this harvest day.

MARJORIE STANNARD

(*b*) Autumn brings the familiar scenes of birds gathering on rooftops and telegraph wires ready to make their way to Africa. The birds go south because there are insufficient flying insects for them to catch. Swifts, swallows and martins are amongst the migrating birds. They breed in Britain and often rear two broods but towards the end of September and in October they fly to Africa. Flocks of swallows have been seen from aeroplanes at 9,500 feet but are also seen just skimming the waves.

Winter

(*a*) Nobody knows
Where anybody goes,
Except when it snows;
Then everybody knows
Where everybody goes.

But where do the birds fly,
Up high,
In the sky?
Nobody knows
Where the bird goes,
Even when it snows.

GILLIAN OLDFIELD (AGED 11)

(*b*) Frost is the quietest thing that grows,
All in a night it comes to leaf
And flower more perfect than the rose
– So firm its stem and yet so brief.
Its seed is quite invisible
Its passing smells not of decay
When in the light the mutable
Thin petals quietly pass away.

They leave no trace but the brown stain
To show where they had sustenance,
They shed no faded whispering train
Of dead leaves in the wind to dance.
Are they compounded only of light
And dying mingle with their source?
Snow in its birth is even as white
But dies with tears and slow remorse,
Less crystal than these fragile spires
Fading like insubstantial ghost
Into the sun's new-kindled fires
That fuse their gold with silver frost.

T. W. RAMSAY

The New Year

Father, we like things that are new.
A new white sheet of paper on which to write or draw,
A new shirt or tie, a new skirt or dress,
A new bike, a new car,
A new crusty loaf,
A new game, a new style,
A new tune, a new scene,
A new book, a new friend,
A new opportunity for fun and service.

Thank you, Father, for this New Year.
For a new chance to begin again.
It stretches before us unused.
You say to us,
'Put behind you what is past.
Your disappointments. Your failures.
Your lost opportunities.
Begin from here.
I make all things new'.

Thank you, Father,
We will look forward, not back.
We will fix our eyes upon the living Christ,
Whom we know as Jesus of Nazareth.
We will walk through the year with Him.
By His help, in His strength,
We will overcome. *Amen.*

J. & E. YOUNG

BIBLE READINGS

Genesis 8.22	—	Summer and winter
Deuteronomy 26.1–4	—	Harvest thanksgiving
Job 38.22–30	—	Weathers
Psalm 74.16–17	—	The seasons are in God's hands
Ecclesiastes 3.1–8	—	To everything a season
1 Corinthians 3.5–9	—	I planted, Apollos watered

Christmas

SEE ALSO:
103a,134

(*a*) It's Christmas again, Lord.
Give us a close-up look at love,
a close-up look at God,
a close-up look
at that ordinary boy
with ordinary skin
and an extraordinary way
of saying God is near,
God is love.

Orbit our earth with love, Lord
with that special power
for those special people
you love.

Merry Christmas, Lord.
Merry Christmas.

NORMAN C. HABEL

(*b*) Christmas is for old and young.
Christmas is for now and then.
Christmas is for all the time.
Christmas is for all.

Christmas is for north and south.
Christmas is for east and west.
Christmas is for everywhere.
Christmas is for all.

Christmas is for rich and poor.
Christmas is for good and bad.
Christmas is for everyone.
Christmas is for all.

DAVID HARDING

(*a*) Is it not true to say that Christmas would hardly be Christmas without shoals of greetings cards of every size, shape, colour and price? A little more than a century ago, however, such cards were unknown. It has been suggested that the first Christmas greetings card, designed by J. C. Horsley, was printed for Sir Henry Cole in 1843. A year later the Rev. Edward Bradley, a Newcastle clerygman, had some Christmas cards privately printed. Or did the idea actually begin with a boy of sixteen, William May Egley, later noted for his skill in illustrating novels by Charles Dickens? It seems difficult to decide precisely who set the Christmas card avalanche moving – and certainly nobody will ever be able to calculate how many Merry Christmasses have been sent by post.

H. L. GEE

(*b*) The lonely couple
All forgotten
Just owning a scooter
Both reporting to the Probation Officer.
No one will care
No one wants to care.

They need shelter
They try every slum
A pub owner offers the bike racks
He thinks he is being kind.

There a baby leader is born
Motor-bike friends bring gifts.
One brings scent
One brings money
One brings a coffin
They speak of life
They speak of death.

TIM WESTWOOD (AGED 14)

Germany gave us the custom of decorating small fir trees for Christmas. In Finland the children sleep on straw on Christmas Eve, and look up at shining paper stars hung from the ceiling. In southern Syria they receive their presents from a small camel, to remind them that the Wise Men travelled by camel to take their gifts to Jesus. Every night for a week before Christmas boys in Gambia go around in processions carrying home-made ships' lanterns. In India the walls of the houses of Christian families are newly washed and painted with pictures of shepherds, the Wise Men and their star.

In Sarawak the streets are waterways, and lighted candles are carried in the boats on Christmas Eve, as the carol singers paddle their way from house to house. In the Moravian church they hold a Christingle service. In Puerto Rico children dress in bright costumes and go from door to door singing carols about the Wise Men. Eskimos in an Alaskan village have a four-hour supper party in church, and then a Christmas service.

In Samoa each village has its own choir, and the people gather outside the pastor's house for the Christmas service, letting off crackers and fire guns at the end as a sign of joy and gladness. Indeed all these customs are expressions of this same joy. . . .

ELSIE JONES

(*a*) Birthdays are for presents,
Birthdays are for fun,
Birthdays are for gladness –
Each year I have one;
But the birthday I like best
I can share with all the rest –
Jesus' birthday is for everyone.

When I have a birthday
It belongs to me.
No one else gets presents
Unless they come to tea;
But the birthday I like best
I can share with all the rest –
Jesus' birthday is for everyone.

When he has his birthday
It is ours to share.
Christmas is for ever
For people everywhere.
So the birthday I like best
I will share with all the rest –
Jesus' birthday is for everyone.

DAVID HARDING

(*b*) Christmas in lands of the fir tree and pine;
Christmas in lands of the palm tree and vine;
Christmas where snow peaks stand solemn and white;
Christmas where cornfields lie sunny and bright;
Everywhere, everywhere, Christmas tonight.

PHILLIPS BROOKS

(*a*) "There are many things from which I might have derived good, by which I have not profited, I dare say," returned the nephew: "Christmas among the rest. But I am sure that I have always thought of Christmas time, when it has come round – apart from the veneration due to its sacred name and origin, if anything belonging to it can be apart from that – as a good time: a kind, forgiving, charitable, pleasant time: the only time I know of, in the long calendar of the year, when men and women seem by one consent to open their shut-up hearts freely, and to think of people below them as if they really were fellow-passengers to the grave, and not another race of creatures bound on other journeys. And therefore, uncle, though it has never put a scrap of gold or silver in my pocket, I believe that it *has* done me good, and will do me good; and I say, God bless it!"

CHARLES DICKENS

(*b*) When I give a present to Jesus
He tells me to give it to you.
I am sure that this should please us,
For it means that He loves you too.

When I sing a carol for Jesus
He tells me to sing it for you.
I am sure that this should please us,
For it means that He loves you too.

When I want to be kind to Jesus
He tells me to be kind to you.
I am sure that this should please us,
For it means that He loves you too.

When I share my Christmas with Jesus
He tells me to share it with you.
I am sure that this should please us,
For it means that He loves you too.

DAVID HARDING

Kaspar: I bring the gift of gold: symbol of man's wealth and glory; the standard by which nations judge their prosperity and power. And yet the symbol too, of human greed and selfishness. For my gift men have killed, man has built injustice and oppression. For this gift man has degraded man. With this gift I offer my hope – that human wealth and resources may be used with fairness and justice.

Melchior: I bring the gift of frankincense: symbol of prayer and human aspiration; the silent longing that makes man lift his eyes to heaven; the inner power that draws us on from what we are to what we ought to be. With this gift I offer my hope – that men across the world will see the dignity that God has given us and recognise the rights of all.

Balthazar: I bring the gift of myrrh: symbol of suffering. Here is the pain of poverty and war. Here the agony of a mother who cannot ease her child's hunger; the father who, with strong hands, has no work to do; the family disrupted by homelessness and the country divided by war. With this gift I offer my hope – that men will learn to share the sufferings of others.

Fourth wise man: I bring my gifts, too: the gifts of the twentieth century. I bring the possibilities of travel, the marvels of communication, news coverage and the speed of life that has made the world a smaller place. I bring the gold of our industrial wealth. I bring frankincense; the rising hopes of men and women seeking peace and love and justice. I bring myrrh: the cry of the poor and the poverty of half the world. And with these gifts the hope that through Jesus born in Bethlehem the world might become one family.

Mother do you see that brightly coloured tree?
People are buying lovely things,
There's holly leaves and paper chains
But what does Christmas mean?

Son, this is the way we plan for Christmas day,
This is the time for peace with all;
Special gifts and friendliness –
That's what Christmas means.

Mother what about war, and all the people that's poor?
Will hungry children get food to eat?
Will soldiers stop their tanks and planes?
Is that what Christmas means?

Yes, just like I say, will be on Christmas Day
Bells will ring and carols sung.
Peace on earth will be the thing –
Until the following day!

CHRISTOPHER DOHERTY

BIBLE READINGS

Isaiah 9.2–3, 6–7; 11.1–9	—	Signposts to Christmas
Matthew 1.18–25; Luke 2.1–7	}	The birth of Jesus
Matthew 2.1–12; Luke 2.8–20	}	Wise men and shepherds
John 1.1–14	—	The Christmas story in poetry
1 John 1.1–4	—	Jesus really did live

Easter to Whitsun

SEE ALSO:

15c,21b,62a,68,
89a,90,104a,134

After his death his disciples began to think seriously about Jesus' life. They soon realised that the courage, humility and sacrifice they saw at his death could be seen throughout his life.

(*a*) The heavenly child in stature grows,
And growing, learns to die;
And still His early training shows
His coming agony.

The Son of God His glory hides
With parents who were poor;
And He, who made the heavens, abides
In dwelling-place obscure.

Those mighty hands that rule the sky
No earthly toil refuse;
The Maker of the stars on high
A humble trade pursues.

For this Thy lowliness revealed,
Jesus, we Thee adore,
And praise to God the Father yield
And Spirit evermore.

J. B. DE SANTEUIL

(*b*) He always had the very nature of God,
But he did not think that by force he should try to become equal with God,
Instead, of his own free will he gave it all up,
And took the nature of a servant.
He became like a man, he appeared in human likeness;
He was humble and walked the path of obedience to death – his death on the cross.

Philippians 2.6–8 (T.E.V.)

(*a*) Trotting, trotting through Jerusalem,
Jesus, sitting on a donkey's back,
Children waving branches, singing,
'Happy is he that comes in the name of the Lord!'

Many people in Jerusalem
Thought he should have come on a mighty horse
Leading all the Jews to battle –
'Happy is he that comes in the name of the Lord!'

Trotting, trotting through Jerusalem,
Jesus, sitting on a donkey's back,
Let us join the children singing
'Happy is he that comes in the name of the Lord!'

ERIC REID

(*b*) Excitement grew to fever pitch,
The army drafted to the town,
Authority must be maintained
And troublemakers be put down.

The city's full to bursting point,
Informers mingle with the crowd.
Peace must be kept at any price,
No demonstrations are allowed.

Now church and state for once agree,
Arrest all suspects without charge!
The individual doesn't count
When vested interests are so large.

He could have stayed in Galilee.
He could have walked unnoticed by.
Instead he rode, the King of Kings!
Hosanna! Demonstrator, die!

RUTH CONNOLLY

CENTURION. Stand up, men. Stand by the crosses. I can still see you, black as it is! What's the matter with you, Sergius? You're trembling all over.

SERGIUS. It's this darkness, sir – it's uncanny. Seems like the gods are angry with us.

CENTURION. That's enough from you, Sergius. Our job is to see that the execution is carried out – never mind our feelings. Anyway, the darkness is lifting now, I think.

JESUS. Eli, Eli, lama sabachthani.

1st BYSTANDER. What's that mean? Sounds as if he's calling for Elijah!

2nd BYSTANDER. (*In sudden pity*) Oh, be quiet you! I reckon he's thirsty. (*To the CENTURION*) Centurion, is it all right for me to push up this spongeful of wine? I can just about reach his lips with it on my stick.

CENTURION. All right. But he's pretty nearly gone.

A SCRIBE. Don't any of you understand your native tongue? He wasn't calling for a drink. He wasn't calling for Elijah. He called, "My God! My God! Why hast thou forsaken me?"

JESUS. (*In exhausted triumph*) It is finished!

SERGIUS. Does that mean he's dead, sir?

CENTURION. No, he's not dead, though he's not long to go now. But (*in admiration*) didn't any of you hear the way he said those words? I've seen hundreds of men crucified, and sooner or later they all crack up. But not this man. He spoke as though he'd won a victory. Listen, all of you! He's trying to speak again.

JESUS. Father, into thy hands I commend my spirit.

SERGIUS. I reckon he's gone now, sir.

J. B. PHILLIPS

Procula. Centurion, were you at the killing of that teacher today?

Longinus. Yes, lady.

Procula. Tell me about his death.

Longinus. It is hardly fit hearing for you, my lady . . .

Procula. Do not tell it all, then, but tell me what he said.

Longinus. The people were mocking him at first, and he prayed God to forgive them. He said: "Father, forgive them, for they know not what they do . . ."

Procula. Was he suffering much?

Longinus. No, lady. He wasn't a strong man. The scourging must have nearly killed him. I thought he was dead by noon, and then suddenly he began to sing in a loud voice that he was giving back his spirit to God. I looked to see God come to take him. He died singing. Truly, lady, that man was the Son of God, if one may say that . . .

Procula. What do you think the man believed, centurion?

Longinus. He believed he was God, they say.

Procula. What do you think of that claim?

Longinus. If a man believes anything up to the point of dying on the cross for it, he will find others to believe it.

Procula. Do you believe it?

Longinus. He was a fine young fellow, my lady; not past middle age. And he was all alone and defied all the Jews and all the Romans, and, when we had done with him, he was a poor broken-down thing, dead on the cross.

Procula. Do you think he is dead?

Longinus. No lady, I don't.

Procula. Then where is he?

Longinus. Let loose in the world, lady, where neither Roman nor Jew can stop his truth.

JOHN MASEFIELD

(*a*) The shops are full of chocolate Easter eggs:
You know we like chocolate, God.

A real egg
Looks as smooth and dead as a stone.
But out of the real egg, so hard and dead-looking,
Comes at last a living baby chick.
Remind me, God,
Why people think that eggs are a good idea at Easter.

Remind me
That when all the friends of Jesus were sad
Because they thought He was dead,
One joyful morning
He was there with them again,
Alive, alive, alive!
And that was the first Easter.

So Easter is the glorious Day, Lord Jesus,
When we specially remember
You are alive and with each of us,
Always, every minute of every day, for ever.
That is the most important thing that ever happened.
Thank You, God, for Easter.

And when we eat our Easter eggs,
Help us to remember why people have eggs at Easter,
And think of You, alive, always. *Amen.*

LILIAN COX

(*b*) *EASTER DAY* Father God, birthdays are wonderful, Christmas is always good fun and the memory of summer holidays lasts all year. Today is Easter Day – a quieter day, a thinking day. Even the very old do not fully understand this day. We welcome Easter Day: its mystery, its promise, its celebration. The Church says that Jesus is in control of death as well as life. Help us to understand. *Amen.*

A grain of wheat dies – to live again

(*a*) Shortly before his death Jesus said: "The hour has now come for the Son of Man to be given great glory. I tell you the truth: a grain of wheat is no more than a single grain unless it is dropped into the ground and dies. If it does die, then it produces many grains."

From John 12.23–24 (T.E.V.)

(*b*) Now the green blade riseth from the buried grain,
Wheat that in dark earth many days has lain;
Love lives again, that with the dead has been:
Love is come again,
Like wheat that springeth green.

In the grave they laid Him, Love whom men had slain,
Thinking that never he would wake again,
Laid in the earth like grain that sleeps unseen:

Forth He came at Easter, like the risen grain,
He that for three days in the grave had lain,
Quick from the dead my risen Lord is seen:

When our hearts are wintry, grieving, or in pain,
Thy touch can call us back to life again,
Fields of our hearts that dead and bare have been:

J. M. C. CRUM

(*a*) Lord Jesus Christ,
In the presence of a king men bow their knee.
You are the King of kings;
We bow the knee and praise your name.

Lord Jesus Christ,
For earthly kings men have given their lives in battle.
You are the King of earth and heaven;
We give our lives in willing obedience to you.

Lord Jesus Christ,
Kings who rule nations expect all to be their servants.
You are King above all nations;
We serve you gladly with time and our abilities.

But we have learned a secret
That you also serve us with love and care.

King of kings!
King of earth and heaven!
King above all nations!
We accept your service with gratitude
And offer ours to you in love. *Amen.*

(*b*) *Like a mighty wind . . .*

In the Bible God's Spirit
is compared with the wind –
invisible but powerful.

Who has seen the wind?
Neither I nor you,
But when the leaves hang trembling
The wind is passing through.

Who has seen the wind?
Neither you nor I,
But when the trees bow down their heads
The wind is passing by.

CHRISTINA ROSSETTI

The Day of the Spirit

We went with a message
And forced them to hear it,
The day that the Spirit
Took over our lives.

He came in a wind that
Went over and through us,
That lifted and blew us
And whirled us outside;
He set us on fire and
We had to declare it,
The day that the Spirit
Came down as our Guide.

He filled us with courage
That nothing would smother.
They looked at each other
And blamed it on wine.
But that was a sneer we
Did nothing to merit
The day that the Spirit
Performed his design.

They shouted us down and
They put us in prison,
But still had to listen
And not shut their ears.
As Jesus had said, we
Were able to bear it
The day that the Spirit
Disposed of our fears.

And why are we talking,
Who live in the present,
As if we were present
That famous Third Hour?
Why, we are their brothers,
Entitled to share it –
The day that the Spirit
Exploded in power.

MICHAEL HEWLETT

BIBLE READINGS

John 15.11–17 — Greater love has no man
1 Corinthians 15.3–7 — Resurrection appearances
Philippians 2.5–11 — Life, death and resurrection

See also end of each Gospel for passion and resurrection narratives.

John 16.7–15 — The work of the Spirit
Galatians 5.22–25 — The harvest of the Spirit

THE CREATED UNIVERSE

THEME COMMENT

God is not the creator who, having fashioned the earth, then stood back, his task completed. He is discovered within creation as well as beyond it. The natural world is forever being created by him and what we call laws of nature are simply descriptions of his creative and sustaining activity. Man is called to work with him. It is increasingly important that man should discover his role in the creative process; the threat of pollution and destruction, if no nobler motive, is driving us to become responsible stewards of creation.

When poets such as the author of Genesis 1–4 or James Weldon Johnson talk about the creation of the world they tend towards an anthropomorphic view. They catch the imagination of boys and girls who think in similar terms and so provide a starting point from which they can move forward. However, we must note the potential danger of such phrases as 'God made . . .' when we apply it directly to an arbitrary sample of creation e.g. a dog, a carrot etc. since it may lead to a crude mechanistic view of creation. Alongside such anthropomorphism we must introduce the concepts of development, growth and evolution.

Living creatures and the natural world excite a wonder closely akin to worship in this age-group. We need not always turn these experiences into traditional language. Wonder is a root of worship and has its own integrity as worship. Repeatedly to formalise the response may well destroy it.

A delight in creation has given poets flights of imaginative fancy. From the Psalms onwards we have allowed ourselves to give voices to the elements, so that they join with us in praising creation.

The vast universe

SEE ALSO:
*20,24c,100b,
103b,147a*

And God stepped out on space,
And he looked around and said:
'I'm lonely –
I'll make me a world.'

And as far as the eye of God could see
Darkness covered everything,
Blacker than a hundred midnights
Down in a cypress swamp.

Then God smiled,
And the light broke,
And the darkness rolled up on the one side,
And the light stood shining on the other,
And God said: 'That's good!'

Then God reached out and took the light in his hands,
And God rolled the light around in his hands
Until he made the sun:
And he set the sun a-blazing in the heavens.
And the light that was left from making the sun
God gathered it up in a shining ball
And flung it against the darkness,
Spangling the night with moon and stars.
Then down between
The darkness and the light
He hurled the world;
And God said: 'That's good!'

JAMES WELDON JOHNSON

(*a*) At the very beginning of all things
God made the universe we know.
The earth lay empty and dead,
darkness blacked out the deep seas,
great winds lashed the water.
God spoke –
'Let there be Light!'
and the world was filled with Light.

(*New World*, ALAN T. DALE)

(*b*) Now creature man has spanned the gulf
For ever fixed between two spheres,
And dared to tread, with pride, the dust
That lights the darkness of his years;
Let him with equal pride take heed
To trample on the dust of greed.

Now Houston's team has sent aloft
Its soaring capsule, wrapped in space,
And pierced the mysteries of the sky
And looked on the Creator's face;
Let man's intensive probe now turn
Where hunger's bloated bellies burn.

How mightily adventuring man
By diligence has stretched his bounds!
New knowledge conquers distant realms
And hope for future quests abounds.
But what of homelessness and tears?
May knowledge not avert *their* fears?

O mighty man! Whose eyes have been
Enchanted by far distant worth;
Have you forgotten? Suffering still
Cries out for conquests here on earth.
Christ spurned the glories far above
To conquer earth with selfless love.

PETER TONGEMAN

(*a*) The tall nose of the shining spear pointing up
Towards the million-dotted, soot-black sky
And bright spheres of luminous light;
A spurt of flame,
A shudder, a shake;
The spheres of night cower.
The rocket presses up
Tailed by a rear of fire.
Ten minutes pass.
A dot of light.
Gone to the stars for good?

ANDREW FULCHER (AGED 13)
Hewett School, Norwich

(*b*) *THE SOLAR SYSTEM* Our sun has a family of nine major planets. JUPITER is the largest and MERCURY the smallest. The planets revolve round the sun and the nearer they are the faster they move. MERCURY, the nearest, travels at nearly 30 miles a second, taking only 88 days to complete an orbit. EARTH (about 93 million miles from the sun) travels at 18·5 miles a second. In this system only EARTH can sustain life as we know it. At 500°C MERCURY is too hot and others are too cold or surrounded by poisonous gases. All the planets are tiny compared with the sun. Added together they make up only 0·13 per cent of the total weight of the solar system – the sun claims 99·87 per cent.

Every star shall sing a carol;
Every creature, high or low,
Come and praise the King of Heaven
By whatever name you know.
God above, Man below,
Holy is the name I know.

When the King of all creation
Had a cradle on the earth,
Holy was the human body,
Holy was the human birth.
God above, Man below,
Holy is the name I know.

Who can tell what other cradle
High above the Milky Way
Still may rock the King of Heaven
On another Christmas Day?
God above, Man below,
Holy is the name I know.

Who can count how many crosses
Still to come or long ago
Crucify the King of Heaven?
Holy is the name I know.
God above, Man below,
Holy is the name I know.

Who can tell what other body
He will hallow for His own?
I will praise the Son of Mary,
Brother of my blood and bone.
God above, Man below,
Holy is the name I know.

SYDNEY CARTER

O Lord of every shining constellation
That wheels in splendour through the midnight sky;
Grant us Your spirit's true illumination
To read the secrets of Your work on high.

You, Lord, have made the atom's hidden forces,
Your laws its mighty energies fulfil;
Teach us, to whom You give such rich resources,
In all we use, to serve Your Holy will.

O life, awakening in cell and tissue,
From flower to bird, from beast to brain of man,
Help us to trace from birth to final issue,
The sure unfolding of Your age-long plan.

You, Lord, have stamped Your image on Your creatures,
And though they mar that image, love them still,
Lift up our eyes to Christ, that in His features
We may discern the beauty of Your will.

Great Lord of nature, shaping and renewing,
You made us more than nature's sons to be;
You help us tread, with grace our souls enduring,
The road to life and immortality.

ALBERT F. BAYLY

BIBLE READINGS

Genesis 1.1–5	—	In the beginning
Psalm 8.1–4	—	The universe and man
Psalm 19.1–4; 148.1–6	—	The heavens tell God's glory
Psalm 147.1–4	—	He numbers the stars

The earth around

SEE ALSO:
30a,70b,78b,79a,b, 80b,82,83,84,85a,b, 102a,b,104b,105a,b, 108a,b,112b,139a, 141a,b,c,d

God of concrete, God of steel,
God of piston and of wheel,
God of pylon and of steam,
God of girder and of beam,
God of atom, God of mine,
All the world of power is Thine!

Lord of cable, Lord of rail,
Lord of motorway and mail,
Lord of rocket, Lord of flight,
Lord of roaring satellite,
Lord of lightning's vivid line,
All the world of speed is Thine!

Lord of science, Lord of art,
God of map and graph and chart,
Lord of physics and research,
Word of Bible, Faith of Church,
Lord of sequence and design,
All the world of truth is Thine!

God whose glory fills the earth
Gave the universe its birth
Loosed the Christ with Easter's might,
Saves the world from evil's blight,
Claims mankind by grace divine,
All the world of love is Thine!

RICHARD JONES

Miracles

Why, who makes much of a miracle?
As to me I know of nothing else but miracles,
Whether I walk the streets of Manhattan,
Or dart my sight over the roofs of houses toward
the sky,
Or wade with naked feet along the beach just in
the edge of the water,
Or stand under trees in the woods,
Or watch honey-bees busy around the hives of a
summer forenoon,
Or animals feeding in the fields,
Or birds, or the wonderfulness of insects in the air,
Or the wonderfulness of the sundown, or of
stars shining so quiet and bright,
Or the exquisite delicate thin curve of the new
moon in spring;
These with the rest, one and all, are to me
miracles.
The whole referring, yet each distinct and in its
place.

To me every hour of the light and dark is a miracle,
Every cubic inch of space is a miracle,
Every square yard of the surface of the earth is
spread with the same,
Every foot of the interior swarms with the same.

To me the sea is a continual miracle,
The fishes that swim – the rocks – the motion of
the waves – the ships with men in them,
What stranger miracles are there?

WALT WHITMAN

Spells

I dance and dance without any feet –
This is the spell of the ripening wheat.

With never a tongue I've a tale to tell –
This is the meadow-grasses' spell.

I give you health without any fee –
This is the spell of the apple-tree.

I rhyme and riddle without any book –
This is the spell of the bubbling brook.

Without any legs I run for ever –
This is the spell of the mighty river.

I fall for ever and not at all –
This is the spell of the waterfall.

Without a voice I roar aloud –
This is the spell of the thunder-cloud.

No button or seam has my white coat –
This is the spell of the leaping goat.

JAMES REEVES

BIBLE READINGS

Job 12.7–10	—	Ask creation about God
Psalm 95.1–7	—	The earth is the Lord's
Psalm 148	—	The world around praises the Lord
Matthew 6.25–31	—	Consider how the lilies grow

Delight in creation

SEE ALSO: *26, 27c, 28a, 30a, 33a, 34, 35b, c, 38, 137, 154b, 159a*

(*a*) Far below him lay the sea, a sea bluer than any sky he had ever seen. The land curved in and out along its edge: in and out, up and down, all green and golden, with here and there the red of flowers too far off to be clearly seen. Down by the sea a road ran along the foot of the mountain, and near it lay villages whose bright colours gleamed dazzlingly. There were trees with many changing tints of green, and over it all shone the warming sun – not white-hot and spiteful and scorching, as the sun had shone upon the camp in summer-time, but with a warm golden loveliness. Beauty. David had once heard Johannes use the word. It must have been something like this he meant. . . .

ANNE HOLM

(*b*) For joy of glowing colour, flash of wings,
We thank Thee, Lord; for all the little things
That make the love and laughter of our days,
For home and happiness and friends, we praise
And thank Thee now. *Amen.*

ELIZABETH GOULD

(*a*) This dirty old brown potato,
Muddy and earthy,
Dug out of the damp soil and clay –
A funny object.
A 'tater', the Cockney would call it,
I wash off the mud and there it is –
Knobbly and irregular,
Pitted with eyes – like scabs.
If I peel it or cut it
I see it is just a lump of wet starch!
Yet if I place it in the ground
Things happen;
A whole chemical factory gets to work;
The eyes sprout strange seeking white fingers,
Reaching down, down,
Sucking in nourishment through tiny hairs;
One or two shoot up, split, spread, get pink
Then green, into light,
Grow leaves, become a plant
Flowering in sunlight.
The soppy lump of starch gets slimy and black,
Dying in its own life –
Come tubers, lots of little potatoes,
Swell, grow,
Provide food and wealth!
What a miracle, Lord,
In this dirty old brown potato!

MURDOCH E. DAHL

(*b*) When I prayed in my heart, everything about me appeared to be pleasing and lovely. It was as though the trees, the grass, the birds, the air and the light were saying that everything prayed, and praised God.

'The Pilgrim'

(*a*) If we knew how to look at life through God's eyes, we should see it as innumerable tokens of the love of the Creator seeking the love of his creatures. The Father has put us into the world, not to walk through it with lowered eyes, but to search for him through things, events, people. Everything must reveal God to us.

MICHEL QUOIST

(*b*) The tree which moves some to tears
of joy is in the eyes of others only
a green thing which stands in the way.

WILLIAM BLAKE

(*c*) . . . nothing's small;
No lily; muffled hum of a summer bee,
But finds some coupling with the spinning stars;
No pebble at your foot, but proves a sphere;
No chaffinch, but implies a cherubim;
Earth's crammed with heaven,
And every common bush afire with God;*
But only he who sees takes off his shoes,
The rest sit round it and pluck blackberries.

ELIZABETH BARRETT BROWNING

(*d*) Flower in the crannied wall,
I pluck you out of the crannies;
Hold you here, root and all, in my hand,
Little flower – but if I could understand
What you are, root and all, and all in all,
I should know what God and man is.

ALFRED, LORD TENNYSON

* *See* Exodus 3.1-5.

(*a*) Some algebraic formulae caught my eye . . . it was part of a paper by a Mr. N. Bohr, of whom I had never heard . . . I sat down and began to read. In half an hour I was in a state of excitement and ecstasy, such as I have never experienced before or since in my scientific career. I had just finished a year's work revising a book on Modern Electrical Theory. These few pages made everything I had written entirely obsolete. That was a little annoying, no doubt. But the annoyance was nothing to the thrill of a new revelation, such as must have inspired Keats' most famous sonnet. And I had so nearly missed the joy of discovering this work for myself, and rushing up to the laboratory to tell everyone else about it . . . twenty years have not damped my enthusiasm.

N. R. CAMBELL

(*b*) Can we not say to the young apprentice who has just learnt the use of a high precision lathe, and is thrilled at his new ability to use so apparently heavy and bulky a machine to prepare a piece of metal to a given shape with an accuracy of one ten-thousandth of an inch, that God is equally thrilled, and that this sheer joy in the situation is not wholly different from that of the angels who behold God's glory and rejoice?

C. A. COULSON

(*c*) Father, there are moments of happiness in my life that I am shy to share with anyone but you: the Q.E.D. of a theorem well understood, the moment when I discover the value of 'x' in an equation, a completed jigsaw puzzle or the discovered answer to the final clue of a crossword, a batch of cakes done to a turn or a finished article in the woodwork room. For these moments of creation and delight I give you thanks, Creator of all things. *Amen.*

(*a*) I like to see a thing I know
Has not been seen before;
That's why I cut my apples through
To look into the core.

It's nice to think though many an eye
Has seen the ruddy skin,
Mine is the very first to spy
The five brown pips within. EDITH KING

(*b*) A seed, so small and dry;
Brown earth where it may lie;
Soft rain, a tiny blade;
Then sunshine, and then shade;
Green leaves, a growing stem;
Tight buds, and then from them
Unfolds, one morning hour,
Perfect, this flower. LILIAN COX

(*c*) There was once a boy leaning over the rail of a luxury liner as it steamed away through the darkness past the fishing grounds of the North Sea. He had been told not to lean over the rails, but he was a spoilt boy without much sense. His father was a rich businessman who had not had time to bring him up properly, and the boy thought he could do as he liked.

Suddenly he leaned over too far and fell into the sea. No one saw him fall so no alarm was given. The boy would have drowned, but a Portuguese fisherman saw him and hauled him alongside his boat. When he woke up, he was aboard a fishing boat, and the liner had gone steaming on without him.

At first the boy tried to impress the fisherman with all his father's money. 'You must take me straight back to port,' he said, 'and my father will pay you anything you ask.' But the men were there to do a season's fishing, and they just laughed. They told the boy – Harvey was his name –

that he could help with the work: swabbing down the decks and cutting up the fish. If he was lucky, they might even teach him to fish.

Harvey never forgot getting his first fish on the line. 'Give him plenty of room. He's a strong 'un,' shouted Dan, the fisherman's son. 'I'll help you.'

'No you won't,' said Harvey, fiercely hanging onto the line. 'It's my first fish. Is it a whale?'

'Halibut, more likely,' said Dan, peering into the water. 'Looks like a hundred-pounder. Are you sure you can manage him alone?'

Harvey's knuckles were bleeding where they had banged against the gunwale. His face was almost purple and he was dripping sweat. But he held on tight and at last the big fish was hauled in.

'It is a halibut,' said Dan. 'Biggest I've seen for a long time.'

Harvey stared at the big grey fish. He had seen halibuts many times in fish shops, but he had never thought how they got them ashore. Now he knew: every muscle in his body ached, but he felt very happy.

When, at the end of the season, the fishing boats put in to port, Harvey was glad to see his father and mother again; but he was sorry to leave the sea. It had turned him from a spoilt boy into someone really worthwhile. Afterwards, when he went to church, there was one verse in the psalms which he always sang loudest of all: 'O ye seas and floods, bless ye the Lord! praise him and magnify him for ever!'

Retold in 'The Morning Cockerel Book of Readings'
from Kipling's 'Captains Courageous'

BIBLE READINGS

Job 37–42 — Awe before creation and Creator
Proverbs 30.24–31 — Pleasure in animals

Conservation and pollution

SEE ALSO:
*63b,77a,
83,152b*

(*a*) Who builds? Who builds? Alas, ye poor,
If London day by day 'improves',
Where shall ye find a friendly door
When every day a home removes?

A mid-19th century London verse

(*b*) Entrusted with an earthly home
Our minds did not create or build,
We live as visitors and guests
Until our years have been fulfilled.

Through centuries, without concern
For all the grandeur and the grace,
We've taken beauty from the earth,
And left it poor, a barren place.

Our carelessness has clogged the streams,
Which once were clear and sparkling strands;
Our industries have blacked the skies
And left a smog on all our lands.

O God, we've been ungrateful guests
Upon this earth, which you designed;
Within our time, help us restore,
Our blighted world for all mankind.

JEAN E. GARRIOTT

(*a*) If everyone goes to the same beauty spot, what beauty will there be left to see? A partial answer is being tried in Britain. Tree-screened car parks are being placed along the Pennine Hills, where country trails and bridle paths begin. Thereafter, access is only on foot. The trails through Germany's Black Forest, or Bruce Trail on the Niagara Escarpment in Canada, allow walkers the enormous rewards of going so slowly that not a leaf, not a butterfly, not a singing linnet or moss-covered stone need escape the eye. But bulldoze in the big roads, extend and pave the camps for the caravans, lay on electricity, build barbecue pits and in a year the linnets are gone, the stones are bare, the leaves grimy, nature's variety dimmed by the clutter of man's present inability to move unless accompanied by an incredible clutter of objects. There are, of course, places for concentrated camp sites. But they should be carefully situated so that they do not destroy the landscape the campers came, in part, to see.

BARBARA WARD

(*b*) Let us proclaim a creed to preserve our natural heritage with right and the duties to respect those rights:

The right to clean water – and the duty not to pollute it.

The right to clean air – and the duty not to befoul it.

The right to surroundings reasonably free from man-made ugliness – and the duty not to blight.

The right to easy access to places of beauty and tranquillity where every family can find recreation and refreshment – and the duty to preserve such places clean and unspoiled.

The right to enjoy plants and animals in their natural habitats – and the duty not to eliminate them from the face of the earth.

LYNDON B. JOHNSON, former American President

(*a*) It's a small planet. And it's the only one we've got at present. Yet at the rate things are going, by the year 2000, if we haven't blown ourselves off, we'll have bred ourselves, eaten ourselves or even washed ourselves off the face of it.

MAX NICHOLSON

(*b*) The world lay quiet;
Not a living thing survived.
Outlines of dead animals and people
Lay strewn across the ground.
Stagnant evil-smelling pools surrounded
Slag-heaps which stood out
Against the horizon.
Mountains of undisposable rubbish
Cast shadows over deserted towns.
The sea, now dead, had lost
Its ever-tumbling waves. Thick oilslicks
Covered its surface and the pebbly beach.
Huge heaps of rusty oil drums
Leaned against the cliff face.
Deserted oil rigs stood sentinel;
Crumbling ruins of a long-forgotten industry.
Pollution came; it conquered; it destroyed.

DENISE SLAUGHTER (AGED 13)
Hewett School, Norwich

(*c*) When we are careless with the beasts, and forget they are God's creatures;
When we are unkind to men, and forget they are God's children;
When we ill-treat the land, and forget it is the splendour of God;
Oh God, forgive us.

ANON

'Mummy, Oh Mummy, what's this pollution
That everyone's talking about?'
'Pollution's the mess that the country is in,
That we'd all be far better without.
It's factories belching their fumes in the air,
And the beaches all covered with tar,
Now throw all those sweet papers into the bushes
Before we get back in the car.'

'Mummy, Oh Mummy, who makes pollution,
And why don't they stop if it's bad?'
' 'Cos people like that just don't think about others,
They don't think at all, I might add.
They spray all the crops and they poison the flowers,
And wipe out the birds and the bees,
Now there's a good place we could dump that old mattress
Right out of sight in the trees.'

'Mummy, Oh Mummy, what's going to happen
If all the pollution goes on?'
'Well the world will end up like a second-hand junk-yard,
With all of its treasures quite gone.
The fields will be littered with plastics and tins,
The streams will be covered with foam,
Now throw those two pop bottles over the hedge,
Save us from carting them home.'

'But Mummy, Oh Mummy, if I throw the bottles,
Won't that be polluting the wood?'
'Nonsense! that isn't the same thing at all,
You just shut up and be good.
If you're going to start getting silly ideas
I'm taking you home right away,
'Cos pollution is something that other folk do,
We're just enjoying our day.'

SOURCE UNKNOWN

(*a*) Each night at dusk the children stood guard at the side of a busy road. They could be seen picking up large frogs and putting them in baskets. As each basket was filled the children carefully crossed the road and emptied the baskets. The teacher present explained that a certain species of frog returned each year to spawn in the same pond. Since the previous season the road had been built blocking their path with the result that hundreds had ended their lives under the wheels of cars and lorries – until the children acted as a human bridge to save the species from local extinction.

(*b*) Recently a soft drinks manufacturer woke to find several thousand 'non-returnable' bottles dumped on his own doorstep. They had been placed there by those who argue that every bottle – plastic or glass – that is non-returned is a further pollution of the environment.

(*c*) Air and water, grass and tree,
Mine and furrow, flower and bee;
These are gifts no man refuses,
Guide us, Father, in their uses,
That man may offer celebration
In each successive generation.

BIBLE READINGS

Genesis 2.5–9	—	The garden
Genesis 3.17–19	—	The human task
Psalm 8.3–9	—	Masters of creation
Isaiah 35	—	The desert rejoices and blossoms
Romans 8.18–25	—	All creation has a purpose
Romans 14.7–12	—	Personal and community responsibility

Animals and birds

SEE ALSO:

59a,b,77b,83, 111b,112a,122a, 149a

(*a*) He was a clever dog, too. David had heard people say a dog was 'as clever as a human being' but that, he thought, was nonsense. A dog was a dog, and a man was a man, and you could not be as clever as something quite different. But a dog could certainly be clever in a doggy sort of way and King was clever. And good.

ANNE HOLM

(*b*) The earth was green, the sky was blue:
  I saw and heard one sunny morn
A skylark hang between the two,
  A singing speck above the corn;

A stage below, in gay accord
  White butterflies danced on the wing,
And still the singing skylark soared,
  And silent sank and soared to sing.

The cornfield stretched a tender green
  To right and left beside my walks;
I knew he had a nest unseen
  Somewhere among the million stalks.

And as I paused to hear his song,
  While swift the sunny moments slid,
Perhaps his mate sat listening long,
  And listened longer than I did.

CHRISTINA ROSSETTI

(*a*) I have thrilled to the notes of a blackbird's song,
The moorland curlew's cry,
A lark's long throbbing ecstasy
Flooding the summer sky.
But the call that stirs my heart,
And sets my eyes alight,
Is the wild call, the haunting call,
Of gulls in soaring flight.

For it calls me afar to the towering cliffs,
And rocks where the great seas break;
To islands lost in summer haze,
Ships with a foaming wake:
Where the gulls in grey and white,
Upborne on tireless wing,
With a wild cry, a haunting cry,
In ceaseless circles swing.

ALBERT F. BAYLY

(*b*) THE HUSKY is one of the hardiest of dogs and a great servant of man. Pulling the sledges of Eskimos, explorers, traders, doctors and the police, the husky was, until recently, the only means of travel at the North Pole. Weighing from 60 to 100 lb. the husky can pull far more than its own weight covering 25 miles a day under normal conditions. Young dogs are hitched in a team with older dogs and thus learn from the veterans. Each team has a 'boss-dog' who can fight any dog in the team and is always willing to show it. The 'lead-dog' is chosen for its quieter character and determination and responds to the driver's voice instantly. It will often make decisions of its own. For example, it will steer the team away from thin ice the driver has not seen or lead the team back home when the driver has lost his way.

(*a*) PENGUINS are always popular at the zoo. There are seventeen different types and the largest and most strange is the Emperor penguin. The female lays one large white egg and, for the entire period of the incubation carries it balanced on her two flat feet managing to waddle along during this period. After hatching, the baby penguin sees no reason to move and spends its first weeks still balanced no its mother's feet.

(*b*) Father, you have taught us that sparrows are under your almighty care; hear us as we remember the animals and all feathered things.

We praise you for the love of those men and women who have worked in the past to deliver animals from much agony.

For fewer ponies condemned to a life of darkness in the mines; for fewer bull-fights; for those societies who minister to the pains and sufferings of dogs, and cats and horses; for the clinics in our land; for all evidence of man's love for animals, we give you praise. Yet we remember those vast numbers who still suffer because of thoughtlessness or greed of man. The animals who suffer slow death in traps to give us furs, the horses who are still butchered at fights to give men entertainment, the stag and the fox which still flee in terror before the hounds to make a day of sport, and for all animals who suffer through cramped conditions in cages and circuses, we pray.

Help us that we may fight valiantly for these, our dumb friends, and make the hearts of men gentle with love for all your creation.

G. S. PAIN (altd.)

(*a*) When God had finished the stars and whirl of coloured suns
He turned His mind from big things to fashion little ones,
Beautiful tiny things (like daisies) He made, and then
He made the comical ones in case the minds of men
Should stiffen and become
Dull, humourless, and glum:
And so forgetful of their Maker be
As to take even themselves – quite seriously.

Caterpillars and cats are lively and excellent puns:
All God's jokes are good – even the practical ones!
And as for the duck, I think God must have smiled a bit
Seeing those bright eyes blink on the day He fashioned it.
And He's probably laughing still at the sound that came out of its bill!

F. W. HARVEY

(*b*) THE CLEANER-FISH. In the Caribbean, Maldive Island and other places 'cleaner-fishes' do the job which a housewife expects from a vacuum cleaner. Small parasites and decayed tissue irritate larger fishes and the job of the cleaner-fish is to work over the fish's body, under its gills and even in its mouth to clear away unwanted matter. Some cleaners invite larger fish to be cleaned by dancing in front of them and fish have even been known to queue up presenting themselves to the cleaners one by one. Whilst cleaning, the cleaner-fish repeatedly flicks its host with its fins so that the larger fish raises its fins or opens its gills to allow access.

(*a*) Zoos are not a modern invention. Archaeologists have dug up plates from the Egyptian Empire of 5000 years ago showing antelopes, cheetahs and other animals. 3000 years ago a Chinese Emperor set up a zoo in his palace grounds. In 870 BC the Assyrian king established a menagerie at Assur. In the Middle Ages kings and rulers kept lions, leopards and bears. The first live giraffe was shown in Germany in 1220 and the first Indian elephant in Frankfurt in 1443.

(*b*) It is seldom that I laugh at an animal, and when I do, I usually find out afterwards that it is at myself, at the human being whom the animal has portrayed in a more or less pitiful caricature, that I have laughed. We stand before the monkey house and laugh, but we do not laugh at the sight of a caterpillar or a snail, and when the courtship antics of a lusty greylag gander seem so incredibly funny, it is only because our human youth behaves in a very similar fashion.

The initiated observer seldom laughs at the bizarre in animals. It often annoys me when visitors at a zoo or aquarium laugh at an animal that, in the course of its evolutionary adaptation, has developed a body-form which now deviates from the usual. The public is then deriding things which, to me, are holy: the riddles of the Genesis, the Creation and the Creator. The grotesque forms of a chameleon, a puffer or an anteater awake in me feelings of awed wonder, but not amusement.

KONRAD Z. LORENZ

(*a*) Black coat,
White blaze,
Soft throat,
Loud neighs.

Four feet,
One head,
Very neat,
Well fed.

Tail long,
Mane short,
Very strong,
Well taught.

Quiet ride,
Good jump,
Lots of pride,
SUGAR LUMP!

ELIZABETH FROSTICK (AGED 11)

(*b*) Thank you, God, for my pet . . .
By his movements may he remind me of your goodness in creating our wonderful bodies.
By his beauty may he remind me of your goodness in creating this wonderful world.
By his dependence on me for his food and shelter may he remind me of your goodness in providing for us.
Thank you, God, for our bodies, the world we live in and your gifts of food and shelter.
May God the provider of good, help us to be providers for the helpless.

From *Time and Again* prayers

BIBLE READINGS

Genesis 2.19–20	—	Man names the animals
Job 39.19–22, 26–30	—	Horse, hawk and vulture
Psalm 104.20–28; 147.7–9	—	Food for animals
Matthew 6.25, 26	—	Birds teach about God

Man

SEE ALSO:
*9b,11c,12,20,22b,
63b,86b,87,95a,
132b,135,163b*

(*a*) Then God sat down –
On the side of a hill where he could think,
By a deep wide river he sat down;
With his head in his hands,
God thought and thought,
Till he thought: I'll make me a man!

Up from the bed of the river
God scooped the clay;
And by the bank of the river
He kneeled him down;
And there the great God Almighty
Who lit the sun and fixed it in the sky,
Who flung the stars to the most far corner
  of the night,
Who rounded the earth in the middle of his hand;
This Great God,
Like a mammy bending over her baby,
Kneeled down in the dust
Toiling over a lump of clay
Till he shaped it in his own image;

Then into it he blew the breath of life,
And man became a living soul.

JAMES WELDON JOHNSON

(*b*) O you shoulders, elbows, wrists,
  bless him, praise him, magnify him for ever;
you fittings of thumbs and fingers,
  bless ye the Lord;
hips, thighs, spine in its multiples,
  bless him, praise him, magnify him for ever.

CHARLES WILLIAMS

(*a*) Help! Help! Help!
What is this world
coming to? –
All I hear of is
Wars, famine,
shortage of oil,
strikes and power cuts.
We live in an environment of misfortune.

Help! Help! Help!
Closer to home
I hear of divorces.
Some of the kindest,
innocent friends
have fallen into
the trap, where their relationship
is only platonic.
We live in an environment of mistakes.

But the world isn't always like this.
Yippee! Three cheers! Hurrah!
Spring is coming and Easter.
People are waiting . . . waiting . . .
I'm finding it a job to tell everyone
how happy and glad I feel.
We live in an environment of celebration.

TINA TUSTING (AGED 12)

(*b*) Who am I? This or the other?
Am I one person today and tomorrow another?
Am I both at once? A hypocrite before others,
And before myself a contemptibly woebegone weakling?
Or is something within me still like a beaten army
Fleeing in disorder from victory already achieved?

Who am I? They mock me, these lonely questions of mine.
Whoever I am, Thou knowest, O God, I am thine.

DIETRICH BONHOEFFER

(*a*) Man is weak. God is strong.
Man needs knowing. God knows all about us . . .
Man is mortal. God is eternal.
Great art Thou, Lord. And greatly to be praised.

J. & E. YOUNG

(*b*) Young as I am, life is so cruel
nothing in life seems to work out well
I have counted my days with hurt and long sufferings
my months and years are well full of labouring.

Life is uneasy, friends are full of untruths
lovers are spiteful, treacherous and deadly
every day as it wanes leaves me disillusioned
I wonder if such will be my lifelight

In dreams and in visions life is so gay-good
my horoscope predicts some brighter futures
but all my hopes and trusts end in ruptures
amidst men's deeds of hurt I go astray . . .

Still on-on I'll strive and struggle
someday, somehow I know my world will settle
for life-lived is like the storms of the seas
sometimes it storms, sometimes subsides. . . .

PAT AMADU MADDY (Sierra Leone)

BIBLE READINGS

Psalm 8 — What is man?
Psalm 102.23–28 — Mortal man, immortal God
Romans 3.10–12 — Man's sin
Philippians 4.10–14 — Facing life with help

Sharing creation

SEE ALSO:
87,91a,92b,
93,95a,109a,
135,149a

(*a*) We all love doing things,
Doing and making,
Cooking and baking,
Painting and drawing,
Hammering, sawing,
Jumping and running,
Joking and funning,
Swinging,
And singing,
And rushing about,
Letting off steam in a shout:
For these and a hundred things more
That You love to see us enjoy,
Thank You, God!
Hurrah!

LILIAN COX

(*b*) If we are images of a creator, then it is up to us to create, and to create good things too. All the things that happened in those distant millions of years were only the beginning. The stars and the Sun, the Earth and the volcanoes, the water and the early living creatures, all these were the beginning, paving the way for the great time when we ourselves could share in the creation of everything that is good and fine.

We live at the end of the beginning. The world will go on into the future, and what is created upon it in the way of good things and bad things depends no longer upon God alone, but on the way in which each one of us does something to make the creation still more wonderful than it was before, helping to fulfil the purpose of the millions of years which lie behind us.

ROGER PILKINGTON

I cannot invent
New things
Like the airships
Which sail
On silver wings;
But today
A wonderful thought
In the dawn was given . . .

And the thought
Was this:
That a secret plan
Is hid in my hand,
That my hand is big,
Big,
Because of this plan;

That God
Who dwells in my hand,
Knows this secret plan
Of the things he will do
For the world,
Using my hand!

TOYOHIKO KAGAWA

BIBLE READINGS

Exodus 35.30–36	—	Man's artistic skill
Proverbs 12.9–11	—	The value of work
1 Corinthians 3.6–9	—	God's fellow-workers

THE WORLD IS A CIRCLE

THEME COMMENT

When, in the middle of the nineteenth century, David Livingstone was exploring Africa, his dispatches home took upwards of six months to reach their destination. A century later, when Americans explored the moon we sat in armchair comfort watching them do it. These two facts are symbolic of our changed view of the world in a relatively short space of time.

Under the pressure of supersonic flight, communications satellites and instant news, the world is shrinking. We have known for a long time that the world is a globe; now it is a circle we can readily encompass.

The Christian responsibility in this revolution is enormous. We have always said that with God as our Father all men are brothers; now we can show it. Wesley's 'the world is my parish' is no longer a vision but a fact and our oft-repeated hopes of universal compassion for all men can now have practical expression in the frequent calamities of drought, flood and famine from which we were once safely insulated by impassable distance.

The world has not only shrunk; its people have visited us. English pavements are trodden by Asian and African feet and children of different race and colour are born amongst us and have rights equal to those of our own children.

This is the generation in which we shall test the sincerity of the Church and other liberal spokesmen who have taught us for so long that the peoples of the world can be thought of as one family with one father and that colour, race, culture and even religion are insignificant against our common humanity.

Our attitudes will teach our children far more than our words.

Round the world

SEE ALSO:

41b, 56a, 86b, 88b, 94, 111b, 114b, 116, 117b, 167a, b, 168, 169a, 171

(*a*)
Let all the world in every corner sing,
My God and King!
The heavens are not too high,
His praise may thither fly;
The earth is not too low,
His praises there may grow.
Let all the world in every corner sing,
My God and King!

GEORGE HERBERT

(*b*) For so many people,
with so many different ways
different languages
and different ideas,
to make our lives so rich and interesting:
Thank you, Father.

Do not let us be afraid of other people,
but help us to think like Jesus
and love them
as you love us.

For the promise
that you will join every different kind of person
in one great family:
Thank you, Father.

We believe you,
we share your joy in this hope for the future,
and we give ourselves in friendship
to everyone we meet,
in the name of Jesus Christ our Lord. *Amen.*

ALAN GAUNT

(*a*) Tell me, captain, merchant captain,
How far have you been?
Travelling in the finest ship
That I have ever seen!

I've just returned from Africa,
Sailing home in haste,
With ten thousand oranges.
Would you like to taste?

I sail today for India,
By the first high tide,
To buy a hundred tons of tea.
Would you like a ride?

Then on to South America –
Brazil and Peru –
For a thousand bags of coffee beans.
Will you join the crew?

PETER TONGEMAN

(*b*) Cheerful songs God's children sing,
East and West their worship bring,
North and South in praise unite,
Redskin, African and White.

Eskimo and South Sea man,
Sons of China and Japan:
Round the world their voices raise
One great Christian song of praise.

ALBERT F. BAYLY

(*a*) The Bible travels the world. Each year the world list of translations and new books shows the Bible to be out at the front. It has been translated into over 1,200 languages. One society alone – the British & Foreign Bible Society – is responsible for nearly 900 of these. These include over 200 full Bibles, a similar number of New Testaments and about 450 smaller parts of the Bible such as individual books. As the publications of the Society declare, 'the Bible is not only a great classic, it is still news, and like news it travels fast and far'.

(*b*) *Madagascar and Britain* – equivalent proverbs from two countries

1. One person on his head can't carry two pitchers of water.
   Don't have too many irons in the fire.

2. The locust doesn't alight on the gate twice.
   Strike while the iron is hot.

3. Scandal is like an egg, when it's hatched it has wings.
   Bad news travels fast.

4. A single tree doesn't make a forest.
   One swallow doesn't make a summer.

5. The tail feathers of a cock are grand even though they come behind the others.
   Last but not least.

COMPILED BY ELSIE JONES

Everywhere we go – whether we travel or eat or sleep, we are indebted to Africa for raw materials. She gives rubber for tyres; latex for furnishing; copper for coins and cables; uranium for power; cocoa, coffee and tea to drink; bananas, oranges, grapefruit and many other fruits to eat; wood for furniture; gems for our jewellery; and string to tie up our parcels. Almost everything we touch throughout the day has some connection with Africa. In addition, some of her people serve us on buses, trains, and in hospitals and industry, and we see many in our towns and cities.

What are we giving Africa in return? Is there a two-way traffic? There are many material things for everyday use that Britain sends to Africa – mechanical vehicles, cottons from Lancashire, tinned food in great variety – particularly milk for babies, good strains of livestock, seeds for farms and school books, too. But the main gifts are less tangible – education, the principles of good government, scientific knowledge of industry and agriculture, and the men and women to carry these over. There is no denying, however, that the first voice to awaken Africa was that of the missionary-explorer, who sought the African as a child of God and introduced him to what were thought to be better ways of life – civilization and education, health and freedom, but supremely to a knowledge of Christ.

WINIFRED WARR

BIBLE READINGS

1 Chronicles 16.28–31	}	All the world praises God
Psalm 145.10–13	}	
Isaiah 42.10–12	—	Praise throughout the earth
Isaiah 43.5–7	—	North, south, east and west
Matthew 28.16–20	}	The gospel for the world
Acts 1.6–8	}	

Friendship circles the world

SEE ALSO:
*86a,b,117a,b,
119,132b*

(*a*)
I cannot hear what people say
In houses fifty yards away.

Yet sitting in my English home
I hear a woman sing in Rome:

Or speeches from a hall that stands
In Holland's silver-threaded lands:

Or flute and horn and violin
That men are playing in Berlin.

Since all the world is small today
And no one lives too far away,

My neighbours need not only be
The folk who live next door to me,

But those who live at earth's far ends
Shall be my neighbours and my friends.

ANON.

(*b*) About half the people living in the world today are poor. In all countries where there are poor people, the local church tries to care by giving help to the sick, the hungry and others in need. One of the ways which Christians in Britain can give support to poor people in other countries is by sending money through the Missionary Societies and Christian Aid. Missionary Societies have always regarded it an important part of their work to care for people in this way. Christian Aid is an organisation which was set up by the British Council of Churches specially to help poor people to help themselves.

From a *Getting to Know* leaflet

If I took a ship and sailed afar
  And came upon another land,
And met with other children there
  Whose talk I could not understand,
  What could I do to let them see
  That friends with them I wished to be?
  I'd smile, and they would smile at me.

Their eyes might be of dancing blue,
  Or brown, or black as ebony;
Their cheeks might be of amber hue:
  They might be dark, or fair as me –
  But all we'd need to try and say
  Would be 'Hello' in our own way,
  And we'd be friends enough to play.

They might have flowers in their hair,
  And cotton gown, or furry suit;
A sari, fez or turban wear,
  In sandals run, or skip barefoot.
  No matter to what land I came,
  In any one we'd do the same;
  We'd all take hands and start a game.

A goatskin tent their home might be,
  A hut of thatch, a snow igloo;
Perhaps a house built in a tree,
  Or made of paper and bamboo –
  With any folk beneath the sun
  I'd feel at home when we'd begun
  To laugh and chase and have some fun.

Instead of trains they might have sleighs,
  Instead of cars, canoes or rafts:
Or travel warm and dusty ways
  In carts with oxen in the shafts –
  Although we'd never met before,
  As friends we'd play, as friends explore
  And want to know each other more.

DORIS M. GILL

(*a*) Of all the happy lands
That wrap this planet round,
Our country seems to us
The finest to be found.
But Hans and Hess and Sved
Elsewhere were born and bred;
And each one loves his homeland,
His fair friendly homeland,
His fine friendly homeland most of all.

Of all the happy lands
That with this planet move,
There's none without its song
Of loyalty and love,
God sets us here and there
To prove all earth is fair;
Then one and all come praise Him.
Folk far and near, come praise Him,
O all the world, come praise Him most of all.

DORIS M. GILL

(*b*) May I be no man's enemy, and may I be the friend
of that which is eternal and abides.
May I never quarrel with those nearest me:
and if I do, may I be reconciled quickly.
May I love, seek, and attain only that which is good.
May I wish for all men's happiness and envy none.

EUSEBIUS
(Third century A.D.)

BIBLE READINGS

1 Kings 5.1–11	—	Friendship through trade
1 Kings 10.1–10	—	Friendship through foreign visits
Isaiah 2.1–5 Micah 4.1–4	}	Friendship through worship

Different?

SEE ALSO:
*9b,16,17,44a,47a,
86a,b,88b,90,147c,
156a,163b,164b*

(*a*) Thousands of different leaves on a tree;
Millions of different waves on the sea;

Different animals, different birds;
Different voices, and different words;

Different stories, in different books;
Different people, with different looks;

I'm not like you, and you're not like me:
But we all belong to God's family.

LILIAN COX

(*b*) *Us And Them*

They moved in yesterday
Them Negroes
We moved to the other side of the street
Then more moved in
Until half the street was black and the other half white.
The street was at war
All except the children.
We were having great fun
But our Mums and Dads were playing
Playing a war of nerves
Waiting for someone to quit.

GUY HARRIS (AGED 10)

Black or white or red or yellow,
people big or small,
strong or weak or dull or clever,
whether short or tall;
each is different to the others
but one Father claims us all.

Each one has his special purpose
in the human quest;
Each, without the other's poorer,
cannot be his best
till he finds his life's vocation
in the love of all the rest.

So we greet the love of Jesus,
by which we are shown
how to live our lives for others
as he lived his own;
by his perfect love united
we can never stand alone.

He intends to make all nations
one great family,
shaping from our variations
glorious harmony;
then earth's praises, undistorted,
will resound eternally.

ALAN GAUNT

BIBLE READINGS

Deuteronomy 10.18–22	—	Care for strangers and aliens
Mark 9.38–41	}	The test is compassion
Luke 10.29–37		
Galatians 3.26–29	—	One family of God
James 2.1–4	—	Rich and poor

Is it fair?

SEE ALSO:

50,67a,b,80a,110a, 120,132b,145b,147c, 148,152b,167b

(*a*) One year's Sunday editions of *The New York Times* use 130,000 tons of newsprint, sufficient to supply all the newsprint used in a year in Bolivia, Burma, Cameroun, Ghana, Guatemala, Haiti, Honduras, India, Indonesia, Iran, Nigeria, Pakistan and Turkey – whose populations total more than four times that of the USA.

ALAN BRASH. FORMER
DIRECTOR OF CHRISTIAN AID

(*b*) There is a family
On West Second Street
Who have no money
Or shoes on their feet,

And everyone laughs
At their old man;
They have one meal a day
Taken out of a can.

There is a family
On North Seventeen,
Who drive around
In a sleek limousine.

Peaches or caviar,
That is their lot,
But they thank no one
For all they've got.

There is a family
Stuck in the slums:
Unfed babies,
Uncaring mums.

Just because
They're another colour
Doesn't mean that
They like that squalor.

SUSAN BROUGHTON
(AGED 15)

In big American cities, streets have numbers rather than names. As elsewhere, some streets are known for their poverty, some for affluence and some for the colour of their residents.

(*a*) Among the perky sparrows in the sun
Was one outsider whom they seemed to shun:
They clearly thought that it could not be right
That they were brown and black and he was white.

They fought for crumbs while he stood all alone
Wistfully watching them, for he had grown
Resigned to segregation, which in time
Had made his different colour seem a crime.

His body was as theirs, his chirpy cry
No different when they swept into the sky,
And he flew after them with the same flight;
But they were brown and black and he was white.

DOUGLAS GIBSON

(*b*) It's a funny old world we live in,
And I don't quite understand;
Why should one man be free
And another be a prisoner,
In the same land, in the same land?

It's a funny old world we live in,
And I still don't really know:
Why should one man have a home
And another walk the road,
Without a place to go, without a place to go?

It's a funny old world we live in,
And at times it's mighty hard;
Why should some people eat
While others round them starve?
For them this life is hard, for them this life is hard.

H. GOODRUM

Inferior

What do you see, Joe –
Just a child from a land across the sea?
Is he starving, is he lonely?
Isn't he like you and me?
Turn around, Joe, walk away,
Someone'll care for him, one day.

What do you see, Joe –
Just a child from a dirty London slum?
Is he dirty, is he sick?
Is he deaf, or is he dumb?
Turn around, Joe, walk away,
Someone'll care for him, one day.

What do you see, Joe –
A mother of twelve with her new-born child?
They'll all starve, but she don't care
Just so long as her baby's smiled.
Turn around, Joe, walk away,
Someone'll care for them, one day.

CHRISTINE BELL (AGED 15)

BIBLE READINGS

Deuteronomy 24.10–16	—	Fair laws
Amos 2.6–8	—	Oppression of the poor
Micah 6.9–16	—	Punishment for deception
Matthew 21.12–13	—	Protest against double dealing
James 2.1–4	—	Snobbery

Sharing

SEE ALSO:

43a, 67a, b, 110a, 115b, 117a, 132b

(*a*) If rich men shared
Their awesome plenty,
Then poor men's plates
Would not be empty.
The rich would find
Themselves content,
And poor forget
What hunger meant!

PETER TONGEMAN

(*b*) I don't like thinking about sad or terrible things, God.
Thousands and thousands of people are, this minute,
Hungry and starving:
Help me to bear to think of them, with You,
For You love them all . . .

Thousands and thousands of people are, this minute,
Without homes, without friends:
Help me to bear to think what this means
To them,
And to You who love them all . . .

Thousands and thousands of people are, this minute,
Lonely, or frightened, or ill:
You care about each one of them –
Help me to care, too . . .

Is there anything I can do to help, Lord?
What about the plans I'm making for when I grow up?
What about the money I spend on sweets every week?
Lord, will You help me to share,
As well as to care?

LILIAN COX

Save the Children

If only it were possible
For all the girls and boys
To have enough of everything
Including food and toys;
What a lovely world we'd live in
Such happiness and joys,
With fun and cheerful laughter
Giving out the loudest noise.

We know the different colours
Of the children far away.
Some are most unfortunate
And some are bright and gay.
Many will go hungry,
And thousands will be ill,
So all the fit and healthy ones
Will help them climb the hill.

Not only those from other lands
Are suffering today.
Many on our own green land
Have not enough to pay.
And so I think we all must share
Our fortune and our wealth,
To bring a little comfort,
Some happiness and health.

TANYA ENRIGHT (AGED 12)

BIBLE READINGS

Matthew 22.34–40	—	Love God and love man
Matthew 25.31–46	—	Anything done for one of my brothers
Acts 4.32–35	—	Planned sharing
James 2.14–17	—	Faith and works
Hebrews 13.1–3	—	Hospitality and visiting

ACKNOWLEDGEMENTS

The compiler wishes to record his thanks to all those whose work is quoted in this book. Where no name appears at the foot of an extract, this is the work of the compiler and the copyright is his.

Every effort has been made to trace authors and obtain copyright permissions. Apologies are offered to any whose work has been used but not suitably acknowledged owing to lack of information and any such errors will be corrected in subsequent editions.

The following publishers are thanked for their permission to use copyright material:

George Allen and Unwin Ltd: 21(a) (*Lord of the Rings*), 131, 156(a) (*God's Trombones*)

Associated Book Publishers Ltd: 23(a), 59(b), 64, 65, 139(a), 150(a) (From *I am David*, published Methuen Children's Books Ltd.), 36(a) (From *Chimney Smoke*) and 154(b) (From *King Solomon's Ring*) both published Methuen and Co. Ltd.

Edward Arnold (Publishers) Ltd: 22(a), 31(b) (*Words for Worship*, Campling and Davis)

Barrie and Jenkins (original publishers: Cresset Press): 14(d)

B. T. Batsford Ltd: 32(b) (*Creative Writing for Juniors*, B. Maybury)

Blandford Press Ltd: 23(b), 28(a), 62(b), 99(d)

Basil Blackwell: 143(a)

Jonathan Cape (and Mrs. W. H. Davies): 30(b), 70(b), 73(b)

Christian Aid: 49(b), 71(a), 158(b)

Church Missionary Society: 11(a)

Church of England Board of Education: 170(b) (From *Together*)

Clarendon Press: 11(c), 22(c), 24(c), 132(a): © Oxford University Press; 32(a), 35(b) (From *Wordscapes* © Oxford University Press); 156(b) (From *Taliessin through Logres*)

Collins Publishers: 15(a), (b) (*The Gospels*), 58, 60; 121(b), 126(a) (*Today's English Version*), 123 (*A Man Called Jesus*)

Conference of Missionary Societies: 94, 167(b)

Daily Mirror: 17 (Daily Mirror Children's Literary Competition)

André Deutsch Ltd: 146(a) (*Only One Earth*)

Evans Bros. (Books) Ltd: 33(a) and (b), 36(b), 56(b), 92(a), 111(a), 173(a) (*Child Education*), 37(a) (*Teachers World*), 79(b) (*Book of 1000 Poems*), 101 (*The Swinging Rainbow*)

Victor Gollancz Ltd: 10(b) (*God of a Hundred Names*)

Granada Publishing Ltd: 9(a), 46(a), 79(a) and (b), 86(b), 87, 91(a), 139(b), 143(c) (*Morning Cockerel Book of Readings*; published Hart-Davis Educational)

Gill and Macmillan, Dublin: 29(b), 92(b), 141(a)
The Guardian: 56(a)
Guinness Superlatives Ltd: 27(a) and (b), 28(b)
William Heinemann Ltd: 42(b), 91(b) (*Livingstone*), 138 (*The Wandering Moon*)
Hewett School (and Lakenham Secondary School), Norwich: 45 (b) 47(b), 73(a), 133(a), 147(b)
David Higham Associates: 15(c) (*The Witnesses*), 46(b) (*Silver Sand and Snow*, published Michael Joseph), 63(b) (*The Word in the Stone*, published Collins)
The Highway Press (Church Missionary Society): 95(b)
The Hogarth Press Ltd: 49(a), 69, 106(b) (*Cider with Rosie*)
The Hymn Society of America: 145(b) (From 16 new hymns on *The Stewardship of the Environment*)
Lutterworth Press: 81, 114(a) (*Interrobang*); 116; 160, 167(a) (*More to Recite*); 165 (*Let's have an Overseas Evening*), 166 (*Two-way Traffic*)
Macmillan: 14(b), 71(c) (*I Want to Get Out*, Aidan Chambers), 16(a) and (b) (*Time to Grow Up*), 102(a) (*Collected Poems*, by permission of Trustees of Hardy Estate)
The Methodist Church Division of Education and Youth: 152
Oxford University Press: 86(a) (From hymn *To God who makes all lovely things*); 112(b); 126(b) (From *The Oxford Book of Carols*), 11(a), 100(a), 155(b) (From *Time and Again Prayers*)
John Paul the Preachers Press: 34, 163(b), 171 (From *New Prayers for Worship, New Hymns for Worship*)
Penguin Books Ltd: 59(a) © Gavin Maxwell 1960, *Ring of Bright Water* (Longman 1960); 77(a), 78(a) © Kenneth Allsop 1970, *Fit to live in?* (Penguin Education Connexions Series, 1970)
Pergamon Press Ltd (Religious Education Press): 25(a) (*With One Voice*)
Routledge & Kegan Paul Ltd: 93 (*Adolescent Boys of East London*, P. Willmott)
Save the Children: 67(a) and (b), 172(b), 174, 176
S.C.M. Press Ltd: 54(b), 70(a) – (From *A Source Book of the Bible for Teachers*, ed. R. Walton), 157(b)
Sheed and Ward: 90 (From *The Flowering Tree*), 140(b) (From *A Treasury of Russian Spirituality*, comp. G. P. Fedotov)
Sidgwick and Jackson Ltd: 153(a) (*Ducks and Other Poems*)
The Society of Authors: 26 on behalf of the George Bernard Shaw Estate; 124, as the Literary representative of the Estate of John Masefield
The Spastics Society: 48
Stainer and Bell Ltd: (© Galliard Ltd): 9(b), 38, 66, 80(b), 95(a), 96(a), 110(a), 122(a), 128, 134, 136
Valentine, Mitchell and Co. Ltd: 12
World Council of Churches: 142(b)

The following authors have also kindly agreed to extracts from their material being included, as follows:

Dr. Roger Bannister: 45(a)
Rev. Edmund Banyard: 80(a)
Rev. Dr. William Barclay: 39(b)
Rev. Albert F. Bayly: 84, 85(a), 135, 151(a), 164(b)
Mr. John Bryant and Mr. David Winter: 14(a)
Mrs. Vera Burtt: 41(a), 42(a)
Mrs. Ruth Conolly: 122(b)
Miss Lilian Cox: 21(b), 61(a), 62(a), 82, 125(a), 143(b), 159(a), 170(a). 175(b)
Canon Murdoch E. Dahl: 140(a)
Mr. H. L. Gee: 115(a)
Miss Doris M. Gill: 168, 169(a)
Mrs. Alice A. Gorge: 43(a), 104(a)
Rev. H. A. Hamilton: 52
Rev. David Harding: 114(b), 117(a), 118(b)
Rev. and Mrs. D. H. Hilton: 13(b), 19, 20, 53(b)
Mrs. Doe Howard (for Peter Howard): 105(b)
Mrs. Gracie W. King: 53
Miss Marjorie J. Martyn: 89(b)
Dr. Roger Pilkington: 159(b)
Mrs. Yvonne Tomes: 77(b)
Rev. Peter Tongeman: 44(b), 50, 68, 83, 108(a), 132(b), 164(a), 175(a)
Canon Westwood: 115(b)
Mr. and Mrs. J. W. Young: 13(a), 74, 107, 113, 158(a)

INDEX OF FIRST LINES

A (P) against a first line indicates that the quotation can readily be used as a prayer or meditation and is included in the Index of Prayers (page 189 ff.).

INDEX OF PRAYERS

Prayers in this anthology are placed under the theme where they most naturally find a place. This index gathers them into more formal categories. A number of the groups contain several elements of prayer, e.g. thanksgiving *and* dedication; these are indicated by an asterisk. Some would more readily be called meditations and in others one verse of a poem might usefully be extracted for use as a prayer. In all instances, however, the first line of the complete quotation is given below.

PRAISE AND ADORATION

CONFESSION

THANKSGIVING

DEDICATION